POOR FOOD FOR THE COMMON MAN

BAUMANN
HATTON
REEVE

POSH:food

A BOOK BY BAUMANN HATTON REEVE

POSH FOOD FOR THE COMMON MAN

OH NO NOT ANOTHER BLOODY COOKBOOK! What's this, three blokes from Essex jumping on the bandwagon trying to be the next Jamie what's his face or Billy no fish?

No doubt the marketing people have found a gap, the focus group says 'Oui' and the advertising budget has been set at a level that could pay off the national debt of Sierra Leone. Well sorry to disappoint, but no!!!

There are no marketing men, the only focus I know about is on a lens and to have a budget first you need to have some MONEY.

This is a book about fun and passion and food; for the guy in the street, in the office or down the pub. It's not politically correct, why would it be? So you! Yes you! The mung bean eating lesbian parading in dungarees, step away from the shelf. This isn't for you, read the title! if you don't heed the warning and this book offends you then good, you deserve it!

This book's purpose is simply to entertain the modern man, raise a smile, get you off your arse and cooking; but more importantly to inspire you to change something in your life for the better. ENJOY!

Day

Contents

29 **Full English breakfast**

39 **Grilled fillet of beef with pink peppercorn and mustard butter**

49 **Moules Á La Mariniére**

53 **Pieces of salmon with armagnac prunes cabbage and Monbazillac**

55 **Red Mullet**

63 **Pancakes with summer fruit and Gin sauce**

70 **Duck with bacon, girolles and foie gras**

75 **Sautéed breast of free range chicken, proper mashed potato, pea and watercress sauce**

81 **Honeybrushed rack of lamb**

83 **Pan fried pigeon breasts with brussels sprouts bubble and squeak and posh baked beans**

84 **Pork tenderloin, calvados apples and mustard Buerre Blanc**

86 **Complicated cutlet of veal with green and yellow beans**

88 **The ultimate tomato ketchup**

96 **Cep and girolle soup**

102 **Profiteroles with custard, dark and white chocolate sauce**

123 **Poire Williams pears poached in armagnac and red wine aperitif**

124 **Prunes in Eau de Vie**

126 **Mint choc chip ice cream**

146 **Pan roasted pheasant**

148 **Salmon and Bacardi**

152 **Bubble and squeak mash**

154 **Rabbit terrine**

STUPID MILLIONAIRE$ range

164 **Gold cornflakes**

169 **Decadent 'left over' vegetable soup**

172 **Pizza**

178 **Banana custard and Champagne**

181 **Vodka ice lollies**

food for thought

Once upon a time, in the grand county of Essex two mates, both highly professional men, got together to have a moan, share their anti-depressants and basically act like a couple of grumpy old men!

These two men were at the peak of their profession. One a Master Chef, the other a top photographer.

Both men adored what they did, cooking grub and taking photos; but hated the political correctness and bullshit suffocating their art.

The photographer fantasised about a culinary photo book, the chef agreed. But both wanted a different angle – in the shape of gorgeous girls!

The chef's name is Mark, the photographer's is Chris and this is the culmination of their dream. Welcome to POSH FOOD FOR THE COMMON MAN.

Owning your own business is what we all aspire to do but it can also be a right pain in the arse, especially when you have to get enough money together every month to pay the staff. This can lead to a very stressful life full of looming deadlines, shrinking bank accounts and twenty-hour days!

The picture of the family on your desk reminds you that you do actually have one, even if they are but a distant memory!

Day in, day out you become so far removed from the job you once loved that you wonder why you put your-self through it all the time.

We found ourselves at a low point, both having worked since our late teens and now nudging forty (Chris likes to remind me the he's not nudging it as quickly as me though!).

My first TV series had gone down a storm and Chris was booked for nine weeks solid but it didn't seem to mean anything anymore.

We needed to take a break and concentrate on what we really enjoy, a distillation of our now supposedly successful careers.

A book! A tiny happening of unbridled passion, fun food photography and friends. No serious stuff, just enjoyable memories with a few mucky chicks thrown in for good measure!

Our idea was to load the van, get down to a quintessentially French gite in the Dordogne. To shop at the local markets, cook the wonderful offerings, photograph everything and to make merriments with our French brothers (all while drinking)!

We hope that the photos inspire you to cook and experiment with the recipes. This food wasn't for show. We ate it all, especially the bloody photographer. Boy did he put on weight!

I couldn't tell you which one is my favourite, but gin soaked pancakes taste fantastic sitting by a pool in the sun, after a hard day's work!

Starter
Aperitif, the first
course

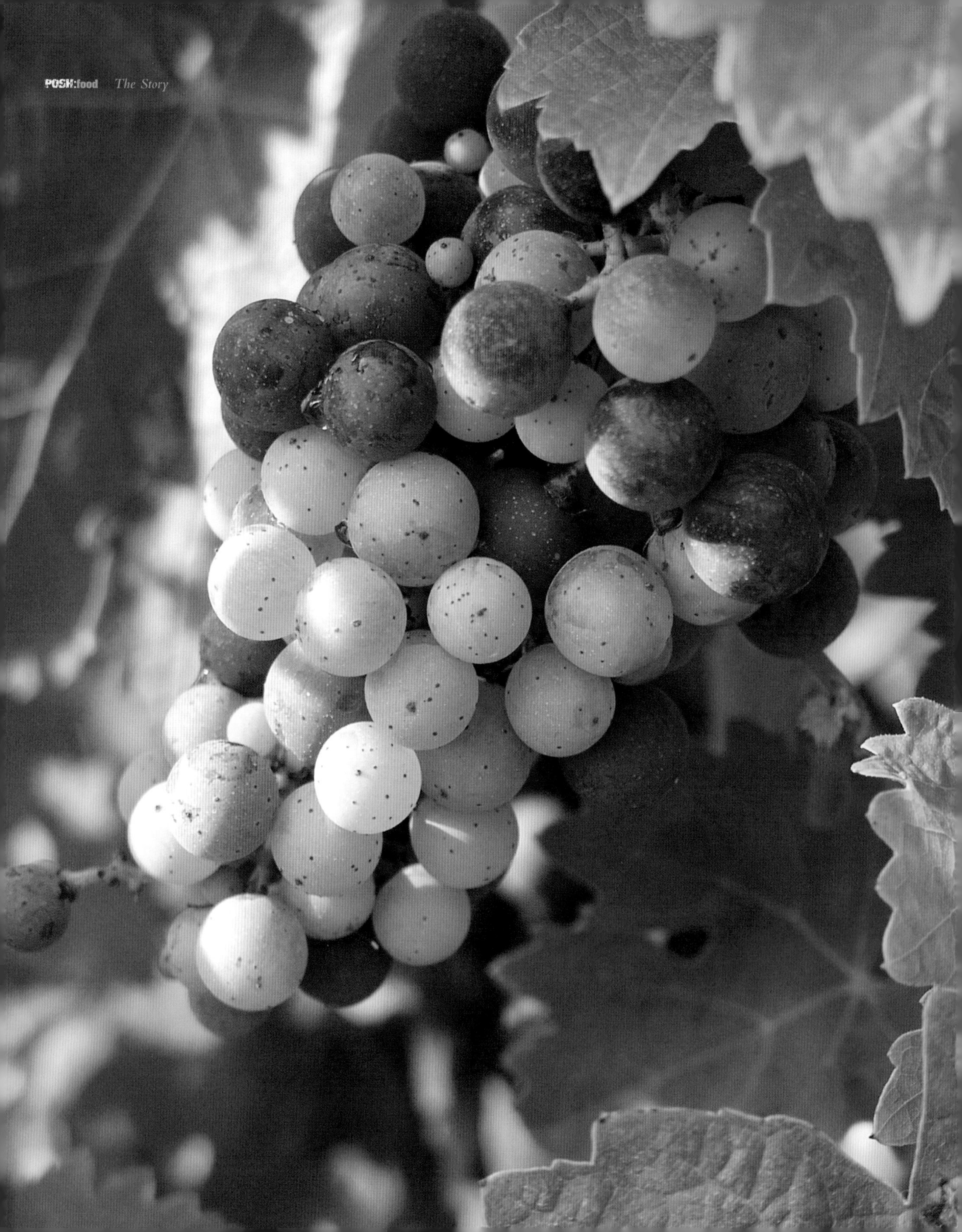

Chris *(gingerbread man)* Reevsie arrived looking stressed and as miserable as sin. Well, he had reason to be – he was at my house at the unearthly time of 3am. We barely exchanged grunts with each other as we drove the dark and drizzly road to Stansted for the 6 something o'clock Ryanair flight to paradise.

"Bloody marvellous" mused Reevsie. "We're the first to check in – we should get good seats on the plane. There's only one other guy in front of us in the aisle." The gate opened. The bloke in front of us turned out to be in the wrong queue anyway.

"Palermo?" he said, "Bergerac" she said, "Dickhead" we said, as we now took on pole position, "Numbers 47-48" she said, "Oh" we said – there were **two** queues.

Our particular flight was piloted by the Formula 1 driver Eddie Irvine, we think, as he bantered on about delays caused by a leaking door and something about a very expensive on board computer in his cockpit that would help him make up for lost time. No matter, we weren't at work!

The doors sprang open and we were greeted by these seductive smells of freshly baked breads, croissants and stronger than possible coffee. We had landed in Utopia, the almost International Airport that is Bergerac.

What a place! The airport building is little more than a garden garage in a field, but it has a bar and the bar serves pastis and all things French. The airport is a thing of loveliness. For a couple of days the world will stop. We have arrived.

Stumbling across the tarmac in the direction of the arrivals garage we sucked in the early morning aromas and the hustle and bustle of this crazy little airport that had itself woken up to greet the first of only a couple of flights it sees each day.

Reevsie had booked a car – a little blue French number which we collected from the lady who became affectionately known as 'The Hertz Girl'. She cracks a kindly smile and poses reluctantly for our photos and even pretends to like us each time we meet. She doesn't believe we are doing a book *(she's probably heard that one before)* and our thoughts are of sending her a copy if ever we succeed in our cause.

Our first port of call is Chateau Monbazillac, an architecturally stunning palace of a building barely minutes from the airport *(must be British heritage)*. After posing for the obligatory stupid shots we sought education and were thrilled by the taste of this gem of a sweet white wine produced right here. We bought a case as a pre-dinner aperitif and moved on.

Now, Reevsie has this horrible habit of stopping the car every two minutes and jumping out to take photos. It wouldn't be so bad, but he forgets to tell you when he's going to do it and I'm sure he forgets which side of the road he's supposed to be driving on. But, somehow we managed to arrive at the little market at Issigeac. It's a breathtaking place, but then so is the whole region, and eventually I found that you become blasé about its beauty.

The morning cloud had by now burnt away and the sun was shining down on these two Englishmen as they continued their journey through Villeréal Rea and into Monpazier – a **bastide** *(we love that word)* with a village market going on; and a lovely girl selling sausages.

As I have discovered over time, I am often the fall guy in potentially dangerous photographic situations. When called upon, it is me who is obliged to keep the subject *(usually a lovely girl)* talking while Reevsie creeps around trying to get the shot. In this case the shot is not of me but of the sausage girl's bum. So there I am talking to her about the merits of saucisson while Reevsie is groping on the floor with his wide angle in his hand. Come on Chris for God's sake, she's going to catch us ....

I'm sure he takes this long to take photos on purpose and I have noted that if the girl's boyfriend is nearby, he tends to stand further away choosing to shoot with a telephoto lens. Good for the shot he reckons – yeah right! *(See photo of sausage girl's bum)*.

Some emergency stops and awful driving later found us at Labouquere. "Stop the car, there's a cow." Peculiar thing really, in the middle of absolutely nowhere these two English blokes are staring at and photographing a beige cow with its tongue out, when along comes a farmer with a perplexed face.

"Americain?" he shrugged
"Oui" I reply, thinking it would stand us in good stead
"Bah" came the reply
"Non, non, Anglais" I said, pretending that I had misunderstood the pronunciation and realising now that he was not so fond of our allies across the pond.
"Bon" he smiled, shook our hands and vanished back into the abyss from whence he originally came. The cow, clearly a photo virgin, stuck its tongue back in, grunted and left.

As I have said, the scenery here in the Perigord region is truly breathtaking. The region is beautiful. Quiet, unspoilt and alluring, the land gives life to wonderful foods, wines and even tobacco plantations.

The markets are inspirational – the people really care. They are proud people in a proud area. To them it matters. Us, we are just so happy to be here. I am inspired, Chris is excited, snapping photos continually and enjoying his art more than I have noticed for years.

Chickens with Knickers

"Yep, this place will do" we thought as we drove through yet another genial hamlet. Screeeeech ….. the little French number comes to yet another emergency stop.

"Did you clock the old guy back there?"
"Who? Oh yeah!"

This was going to be a bit tricky. We had spotted a man of great character and despite his rather grubby trousers we wanted his face in the book. The only trouble was that he was almost alone in this little village. We couldn't just get the shot and go. Reevsie started shooting everything with a view to capturing him nonchalantly a bit later on. How funny was it when a local lady came out of her house to see why he was taking photos of her washing line (surrounded by chickens) in the soon to be famous photo named 'Chickens with Knickers'. She clearly assumed that the ginger one was kinky. Me? I think she's right.

Meanwhile the old boy just stared our way almost encouraging us to talk with him. His name is Robert. Robert is a man who sits on the same stick outside his wonderfully tumbledown house each time we drive by. Robert raises his hand and waves to us each time our hooting disrupts the equilibrium of his peace. Robert clearly thinks we are mad. Robert is probably right.

Eventually we arrive at the Hotel that Reevsie has been boring me about for months. It is 'Le Vieux Logis' or the old lodge in Trémolat. Now this Hotel is special. So special in fact that Chris and I struggle to pronounce its name, so from now on we shall refer to it as The Shed.

The Shed is marvellous, the Shed is opulent, the Shed is one of those perfect places that you think you are not good enough to be in. It is full of aristocratic Americans, British Brigadier types and now a couple of English men, in comfortable Fat Face gear, that are on a mission. A mission to live and re-discover themselves, their art.

The Shed is tucked away in the tiniest of quintessentially French villages, with perfectly manicured gardens and a lovely swimming pool. It is the perfect place to bring your wife or lover or whoever to indulge in a dirty weekend. But I've ended up with Reevsie and he's ended up with me, so I guess we'll have to make the best of it!

With promises of returning with our wives next time, we are taken to our bedroom – a sumptuous little country cottage set in the gardens of this great place. Chris had asked his wife Rachel to book us a twin room, modestly priced. We were happy to see that she had almost got it right – only trouble was that she had booked us in to what we assumed was the Honeymoon Suite, complete with a heart shaped headboard over our double bed!

The centime dropped. No wonder Clare and Estelle (the charming receptionists) had looked at us knowingly. Still this is France after all.

The best thing about our new found love shack was the toilet in the room adjacent. It has these huge doors which literally open up fully onto the manicured gardens where guests meander enjoying 'Amuse guelle' and pre dinner glasses of fizz.

Now it was my turn to take a staged picture of Chris on the bog, and I took as long as possible setting up the camera hoping that a guest would walk by and catch him. Alas, I was disappointed. There will be other times matey.

After a little nap (battle lines drawn on the bed) we went for a swim and a lounge around the pool. This is work after all and we need to prepare ourselves for a hearty dinner.

We then boldly introduce ourselves to the Chef de Cuisine, a great guy who we have come to know by the name of Vincent.

Vinnie boy wasn't really interested in chatting with us to start with and I do know that from a Chef's perspective, some customers can be incredibly boring to talk to. Harder still for Vinnie, who doesn't speak a word of Blighty.

After some explanation and well mannered conversation, Vincent thawed quite well; advised us on what to eat for dinner then disappeared into his engine room, where he (as do I) feels most comfortable.

His suggestions were not wrong. That evening we munched our way through some of the greatest food we had ever eaten. The Menu Gastronomique offered us more courses than I can remember, of really exquisite delicacies.

The scenario was almost unimaginable. The two boys from the Honeymoon Suite sitting on white lace chairs in the warm night air in the gardens of a beautiful Chateau in deepest rural France.

Served by meticulously attired and stunningly knowledgeable staff, we apologetically opted for beer with our Foie Gras.

Throughout this magical evening, surrounded by blazer wearing Brigadiers and their wives; Chris and I enjoyed copious amounts of lager and sweet white Monbazillac wine, to rinse down our fine offerings.

Ironies are funny things. My wife Fiona called. I quietly picked up my mobile phone and as we sat by this beautiful little stream trickling away in front of us, struggled to hear that her camping break away with our girls had had a hitch. It had been raining incessantly at home, so they had evacuated their temporary lodgings in pursuit of fish and chips.

Chris and I pondered this for a few seconds, tried diligently to summon up sympathy and then exploded into helpless laughter!

Reevsie then pulled out his masterpiece of planning ingenuity, a Dictaphone. From now on we would plan our book, our journey and our mission on a Dictaphone. We retired back to our love nest where battle lines were once again drawn through our bed.

The following morning-ish we met the director of The Shed – a man of sartorial elegance, great grace and presence. Monsieur Frederick, whom we now endearingly refer to as 'Freddie Boy'.

We told him of our plans and desire to write a book, and asked if we could use The Shed (we didn't say that to him!) to take some photos, have the Chef "knock up some tarts" and generally get in their way next time we came back. "No problem" he said and with that we left with thoughts of Freddie Boy reminding us of Serge in one of those Beverly Hills Cop movies.

Lunchtime found us at a Mediaeval Market near Cadouin. In Perigord you know when it's lunchtime 'cause the Restaurants close. But we filled ourselves with some pretty awful mediaeval, pasty things that were filled with duck and stuff and Chris took pictures of the less than mediaeval but no less gorgeous dancing girl.

Now I have forgotten to say that Reevsie's father-in-law and better half have a gite out here. They were delighted when we made plans to visit them some days earlier as we knew that they would be down here for a few days.

We made our way to their farmhouse and were greeted by a startled Tony who had completely forgotten that we were coming to visit. Never mind; we had a chat, a tart, a look around, a wee and left.

Tony and Jane kindly offered to let us stay in their gite, should we decide to go back and pursue our mission and what a place it is. Absolutely in the middle of nowhere. Next door belongs to the lady that produces Foie Gras and that's it! – fields, tobacco plantations, chickens and beauty.

The kitchen is a cook's dream – a huge, high ceilinged affair with modern appliances. The gite is a photographer's dream – character and composition everywhere. The swimming pool shimmering invitingly through the shutters of the kitchen window would help to inspire me with the grub and Chris with the snaps.

Driving back with emergency stops in Beaumont to photograph dogs on roofs, we are both brimming with enthusiasm. We want to start now - can't wait - and the drive over the Dordogne has just left me with no further expletives to describe the splendour and energy of this place.

We finally arrive back at the airport and are welcomed by a sudden storm and torrential rain. Great - we have to fly back in this. Still we are greeted by our old mate the

Hertz Girl (must ask her name) who checks out the car which is, incredibly, free of any scratches or dents. Well done Reevsie. She really doesn't believe that we are going to write a book, and reluctantly poses for another quick photo. By now our Hertz Girl has stopped the rain from falling, and the day is cheering up once more.

Queuing at the passport control for one of only two flights out today, I suddenly have a brilliant idea.

"Chris mate, let's swap Passports and see if they notice." "Ok mate, you go first."
Now I know that Reevsie has got a cunning plan. He wants me to go first so that he can act all innocent and say "Oh look mate; here is your passport. I must have picked it up by accident."

The trouble is that the control guy looked at Chris's passport, looked at me then waved me through! Reevsie lost his bottle. "Mark" he shouted as I was marching through to departures "here's your passport, we must have made a mistake." The control bloke called me back, looked again at Chris's passport - the one that I had been holding, then looked at me and pointed to my hair. He then pointed to Chris's hair, laughed and waved us through. He no doubt thought "Bloody English idiots".

Chris thinks that I look like Adolf Hitler in my passport photo. I think he looks like a Ginger tosser!

Back on the plane with Eddie and we had time to reflect on the most incredible couple of days away.

Our recce had stimulated dead thought cells and neither of us could wait to start on our journey to write our book. We needed to get back here as soon as possible.

Second course

Dinner, the main meal

Tarts and truffles.
Day One; the Road Trip

It's Tuesday the 22nd September and the alarm wakes me with some crap song that's now going to be in my head for the rest of the day. The clock reads 4am it's cold, wet and windy and I don't want to get up. Oh God where am I today? I bet it's Reading, I hate the M25. Why can't I be going to Cambridge instead?

Just when that song is getting really annoying the realisation suddenly dawns on me, I'm going to the Dordogne with my mate Mark to photograph food. Fantastic! I wake the wife to tell her the good news.

Meanwhile 15 miles away in the tiny, picturesque hamlet of Feering; Mark is kissing the floor of his house, having already kissed his beautiful wife and daughters. For some reason, known only to himself, he is now kissing the doorstep of his beautiful house. He then steps into the truck, loaded with half a restaurant and sets off with a grin as big as the proverbial Cheshire cat's.

At 4.30am the truck and still grinning occupant arrive in Colchester. As usual I'm not ready and all the gear is in piles on the dining room floor (including the other half of Mark's restaurant that I've nicked for the trip). We're convinced that CJ (the chef at Baumanns Brasserie) and the boys will only be able to serve haricot en tomate sur toast for the rest of the week. All we left them was the Breville!

My wife Rachel (pronounced Rachelle) greets Mark at the door with that look of resignation that your wife has after you've got her up at 4am then goes off to make tea, while the pair of us load up the truck with the remainder of the restaurant and half my photographic studio.

By five we are ready. It's now my turn to kiss my beloved Wife and MG before setting off to photographic nirvana and by that I don't mean Dover!

The mood in the truck is buzzing. It's the same feeling I used to get when I went on holiday 20 years ago with my Mum, Dad and Andrew my older brother. The sense of adventure mixed with the unknown. It's hard to explain but a vivid memory for me nonetheless coupled with the fact that our wives have allowed us our mid-life crises several years early and we get to leave the rat race, if only for a week. Admit it, we all wish we could do it.

I'm already hungry, a recurring theme you'll notice throughout the trip and Mark delights me with the news that we are having a fry up at his Mum and Dad's near Dover. NICE!!!
"Although Dad forgot to buy the mushrooms" he adds. Bugger, my favourite, I make a mental note to reprimand his father for this geriatric oversight.

Preparing Breakfast
a thing of beauty

The English Breakfast
a thing of beauty

Fried Breakfast
Serves: 2

Now I don't really think that cooking this wonderful national gem from our fine island needs any explanation. I really believe that this fine dish should be taught in school. Anyway, the photo is an indulgence (as with most of the book) and hopefully a stimulant.

Here is what you need to feed 2 fatties:
2x Flat mushrooms (nice and dark underneath)
2x Large potatoes (waxy if poss) (sauté)
2x Plum tomatoes (cut in half)
4x Thinly sliced back bacon (rindless)
2x Pork and leek sausages
2x Free range eggs
2x Slices black pudding

Sauté potatoes
2x Large potatoes
    A tablespoon of duck fat (if possible) otherwise dripping or olive oil
    A lick of good butter
    Sea salt and ground black pepper

You are forgiven for not knowing how to sauté potatoes, so here is a little help.

What you need to do to it:
1. Wash the skin of the spuds and boil them in their skins until they are half cooked. Allow to go cool.
2. When cold, carefully peel off the skins and cut the potatoes into slices (about the thickness of a lady's little finger).
3. Heat the duck fat in a frying pan – just warm then place the spuds in the oil. Cook for 4 or 5 minutes gently moving the pan so that they don't burn or stick.
    When golden in colour flick over and cook for a further couple of minutes till done.
4. Season with sea salt and crushed black pepper.

During the making of this recipe, people kept asking where the baked beans were. Well, I don't like baked beans but if you do …… be my guest!

Our ideas for the book begin to emerge in the two hours it takes to drive to Saltwood. The sun is out, always a good start for any trip.

We are met enthusiastically chez Baumann by Mark's dad (John) and are hustled into the house for what I hope will be a gastronomic breakfast. I delight Mark's mum (Brigitte) by taking her photo, still in her dressing gown, so early in the morning. I'm sure one day she'll thank me for this! "Start as you mean to go on" I say.

The Breakfast is FANTASTIC (even without fried mushrooms). It's quite obvious to me that hospitality and cooking are imbued in every part of this family's life, the sort of service you only dream about but very rarely get.

But before I forget where I am, Mark's mum disappears upstairs muttering something about Christmas presents. Remember it is September!!

Mark has realised he's forgotten his fleece and his mum is going to give him his present early. Now there are times in a man's life where you should be supportive of your friends in their hour of need! This isn't one of them. "NICE JUMPER" delivered in the most sarcastic tone I can muster, I'm shot the look of death as Mark - just short of his 40th birthday - is reluctantly being dressed by his mother and looking like a scolded teenager again. I have a sense of foreboding that maybe my parents will embarrass me as much before this story ends, so I don't push it.

It's nearly 8.30 and with stomachs satisfied it's time to move on. Now I have driven many cars in my life from Minis to Porsches but never a Mitsubishi L.W.B. Tonka toy, but here's my chance. I can see the attraction in owning one of these - the high view point, the practicality of moving kitchens and restaurant in the back and the fact that you look like the Marlboro Man (which I don't!!)

The handling isn't what you call sporting as I find out all to soon by turning into a corner understeering wildly to the wrong side of the road and passing the turning to Dover as I do so. MG it ain't!!! After Mark's laughter and sarcasm die down I decide to adjust my driving style to a more leisurely pace. That akin to the school run!

We find ourselves queuing for an earlier ferry and although it's now really sunny it's also very blustery and the concierge tell us it's at least force 7 out there. I hate rough seas, I'm a bit of a landlubber really, Mark on the other hand doesn't care. He's spotted half a dozen Aston Martins lined up next to us, and we gawp like the poor people we are. Unfortunately we don't notice our queue has moved on and we are holding up the traffic. As we get to the end of the row the ferry guy looks pissed off and makes us wait to the end. Trouble is there are three ferries docking and we get confused as to where we are supposed to be going. We don't know if we are on the right one until rather embarrassingly we have to ask! (Zeebrugge anyone!)

We find the first of many cafés and order two over the top coffees with marshmallow and cream, obviously dropping our Marlboro Man personae for a while. The crossing is rather uneventful, apart from Mark having one of those embarrassing moments in the gents (no it's not size related). Half way through the journey Mark disappears to the loo. While standing by the urinal the intercom crackles to life "Will passengers on the Channel Cruise stay aboard the ferry when we reach Calais, as we will be returning to Dover within the hour". Stifling a grin he turns to the guy next to him and says "Why would people want do that? Sad bastards". "Because we thought it would be a nice day out." he replied, in a disconcertingly deadpan voice A few seconds later Mark appears looking pale.

I point to the intercom and say "why would people want do that? Sad bastards."

We disembark at Calais and the butterflies in my stomach reach a crescendo as at last the real journey begins. Only another 600 miles to go.

I'm driving as far as Paris and Mark is navigating. Just out of the port he stares blankly at the map and rather unreassuringly says "There's a lot of shit out here". Closing the map we both agree just to follow the signs for Paris and then work it out when we get there.

It's now 3 o'clock and we're on our way to Orléns. Paris was remarkably easy to navigate - we just followed the signs for Bordeaux and didn't look at the map once. I may knock the French for most things but you have to say their roads are pretty damn good. I imagine this is partly due to the contributions from the RAF and Luftwaffe 60 odd years ago.

Our first stop was at a service station near Lens. The food looked quite appalling. What we would have given for a Little Chef and two Early Starters! We even took pictures of the carrots festering in what can only be described as orange microplasm.

We decide on ham, chips and béarnaise sauce as the safe choice and move to the checkout where the girl, recognising our now honed Marlboro Man look, asked us if we were routiers? Looking at each other then at the sign that read 'routiers 23% discount' we say "Uh oui" in our best Jean Reno accents (Leon/Godzilla/Big Blue). We wonder as we tuck in to our surprisingly satisfying meal, if we have just joined some religious, French gay bikers cult or even worse Presidents Chirac's fan club. It's only on closer inspection that we find out that we've now become TRUCKERS.

BORD

IRE DE C...
05.49.02.72...
TARTE DU MOIS   2.30
TARTE POMMES   2.30
GRAND NOIR
GRAND NOIR   2.2
2 X 1.10   -2.39
ali 5.5   10.21
ROUTIER PDJ. 23.00%
Total   10.21
                                10.21

Scenes of Smokey and the Bandit and convoys start to appear as apparitions and we decide to hit the road once more with delusions of grandeur at one with our fellow routiers.

Now driving long distances is boring, there's no getting away from it. There's only so much introspective thinking about life, loves, the universe and highbrow political topics before the talk turns to tits and rest areas called 'air de mong'.

Six hours since we left Calais and we're travelling at a steady 80 mph (legal on French roads!) without any thought for our fellow man or anyone else for that matter. A Merc driver cuts in front of us from the fast lane nearly taking the wheel arch off in the process. As it's me who's driving at this point, I flash him to let him Know "that wasn't cricket!!" His response is to slam on his brakes and swear at us. I don't believe his words were an invitation to enjoy his country's scenery. This ignorant French man obviously doesn't realise he is pissing off a couple of Essex truckers. If we had an HGV we would have probably rammed the bastard but instead we give him the birdie, drive beside him and give him an invitation to view our country's scenery because it's a lot more colourful than his!! Mark also threatens to show his arse but the guy has got the message and legged it. After the few minutes of alpha male antics we settle back to highbrow political debate – or was that tits?

It's evening, and time for another break on the A10 and we stop at the beautifully named 'Jardin de beouf'. As we drive in we realise that everyone looks of Arabic descent, fellow travellers and staff alike. Mark remembers his chef CJ saying that there is a big immigration debate/problem raging in France at the moment as there is at home, especially in areas around 'Tours', his part of the world. The upside for us, of this cultural and religious diversity is that everyone seems to be moving outside with prayer mats. We hurry inside, hoping to miss the crowds. Fantastic no queues. We rush to the café, not a soul in sight, we order coffee and apple tarts with our now mandatory 23% discount and ponder. Maybe there is a god.

Back on the road yet again, the light is now fantastic. I start to photograph everything in sight inside the cabin: Mark driving, air freshener, watches, the bugs on the windscreen, which we're going to have to clean off again. I've just photographed yet another bridge and decide to put the Leica down before I run out of memory and Mark follows through with his threat to "shove it where the sun don't shine!!". That'd be road rage then?

We are eating up the miles now – 700 in total. Several fuel stops and Oasis CDs later and we've still got hours to go and now the sun is going down. We were hoping to reach Bordeaux by nightfall, but the traffic is getting heavy and we're both tired. Still, morale is high and we're still talking to each other which is a plus. Unfortunately I discover a rather disturbing fact about Mark, he is the world's biggest Haircut 100 fan and to prove it he starts to recite "fantastic day" a capello. This is going to be one long journey!

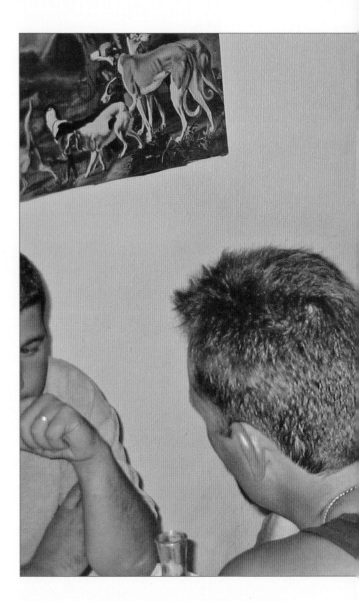

We reckon we're still a couple of hours away and are starting to feel hungry again. It's been a long time since we had our ham and chips and we have no idea where we are, but like a beacon in the night Mark spots a neon sign that says 'Restaurant'.

It must be nearly 10 o'clock. Surely it can't be open? As we turn in to the extremely wide entrance we see about 200 HGVs all neatly lined up in rows. It's a truckers stop, open all hours. "Je suis un Routier" we shout, excited at the chance to eat a hearty French casserole with our trucker comrades. Okay, so the Mitsubishi pick up truck looked a bit pathetic next to all the Scandias and Volvos but we are sure, as fellow Europeans, we will be warmly welcomed. We burst into the bar just as Ryan Giggs of Manchester Utd rockets a ball into the back of the French team's goal and a collective sigh hits the roof. "Bonsoir" said with the usual franglais accent is met with a stony, slightly hostile silence.

Rather sheepishly we make our way to the bar and ask the pretty barmaid for two beers and whether they are still serving food. Without a word two large glasses of beer are plonked in front of us along with two dockets, "23 euros" she says. Bloody hell, that's a bit steep for two beers! With further conversation we find out we've paid for food as well and are sent down the steps to the restaurant. Pit would be a better word. As we enter we see it's full of the Village People minus the policeman, all smoking Gauloises, 40 eyes looking menacingly our way, deciding who would have the pretty boys first. The waitress looked relieved.

We sat down at one of the trestle tables trying to look manly and confident but in reality looking like a couple of Essex boys, out of their depth, trying to give off that "don't fuck with me" vibe but failing horribly.

The menu on the table is not exactly what we were hoping for. Coq au Vin and Boeuf Bourguignon it isn't! It lists 'veal head, tripe and sausages made of duck gizzards' to name but a few. We recognise steak en frites and order, hoping all the French truckers (that's not a spoonerism) hadn't got there before us..

As we came into the Pit there were tables and fridges with fruit and olives to which we help ourselves. But before Mark sits back down he tells me he's going to take a photo, with me stuck in the middle. "No one's going to believe this place" he whispers - "Don't worry, I'll do it so no one notices". As I sit down I realise the flash is on auto. I try desperately to get his attention but it's too late. He presses the button "Wallop" the flash discharges on full power and everybody stops talking, turning round to look.

Any credibility we might have had has now evaporated quicker than a battlefield full of Frenchmen.

I turn to the rough, bearded guy next to me and say "Je suis un Englishman". He duly laughs and and they all carry on with their business. Plan B was to leg it.

The steak and chips arrived and I have to say they were bloody good. Maybe the fact we were both starving has influenced our judgement. It certainly influenced one of our upcoming recipes.

Time as ever is moving on and we are keen to continue our journey. After browsing the 20" flick knives on sale by the bar, we bid farewell to the waitress and depart, taking a few photos of the neon signs as we go.

Back in the van we re-live the experience, both of us in hysterical laughter, at the amount of clichés we had just lived through!!

It's nearly midnight and we're on single carriageway roads now, going cross-country toward the gite "Road to nowhere" is on the stereo, definitely the anthem of this trip!! But the end of the journey is in sight, so spirits are still high. 799 miles and twenty hours later we arrive at Labouquerie. We are both knackered but still have enough energy to unload the van, pick a room and crash. It's the end of Day One and tomorrow the fun begins.

Grilled Fillet of Beef "chez trucker Eric" with pink peppercorn and mustard butter

Serves:2

Here is what you need:

2x Fillets of beef (well hung – not like Chris!) 250g
4x Large potatoes
1 Teaspoon of pink peppercorns
3 Cloves crushed garlic
100g Unsalted butter
1 Tablespoon coarse grain mustard
4 Large flat mushrooms
Salt and pepper
Cooking oil (for frying chips)
Butter (for cooking)

First make the butter

What you need to do to it:

1. Soften the butter in a bowl.
2. Crush garlic and crush peppercorns.
3. Mix together the garlic, peppercorns, mustard and salt and pepper with the butter.
4. Roll like a fat cigar and place in fridge to set hard.

And the rest

1. Cut the potatoes into posh chips and heat fryer.
2. Season the fillets with salt and pepper and "sear" in a really hot pan (with melted butter and a little cooking oil).
3. When the fillet is brown all round place in a hot oven (220°C fan assisted/Gas mark 7) for between 5-12 minutes depending on level of doneness (rare to well done).
4. Place posh chips in fryer.
5. Heat a fry pan with a knob of butter and oil.
6. Season mushrooms and fry in the pan until just soft.
7. Get your fillet out, rest it properly.
8. Season the chips with salt. Cut a large lump of butter and place it on top of the meat, garnish with the mushrooms.

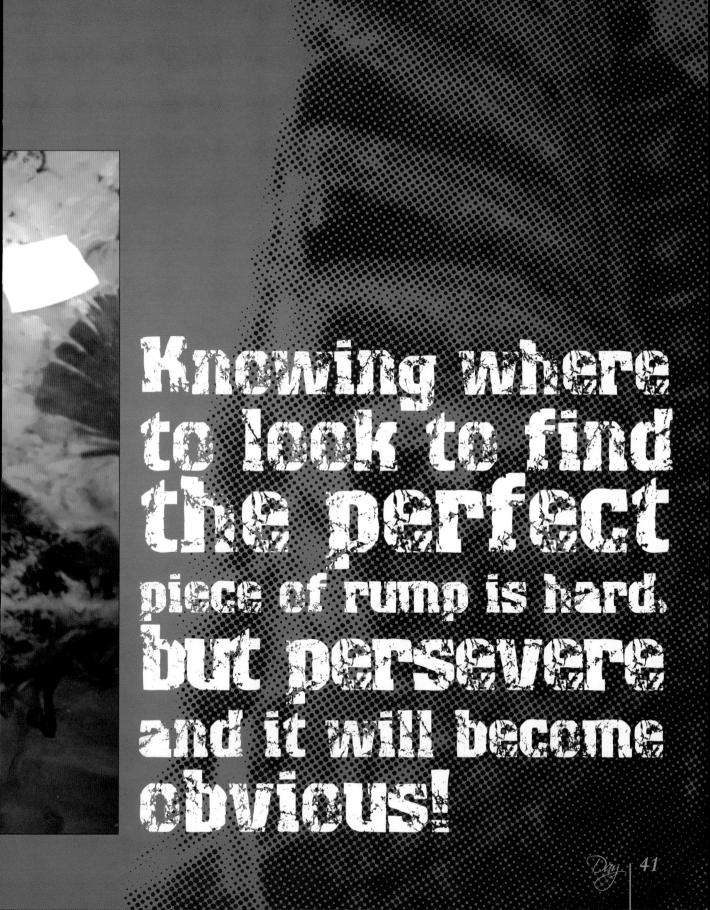

Knowing where to look to find the perfect piece of rump is hard, but persevere and it will become obvious!

Chris's mouth tastes like a bird shat in it (quote) – maybe that's a reflection on the type of girl Reevsie used to date!

You know that horrible feeling that comes over you after a long haul flight – the sort of smelly breath, out of body experience that hits you after crossing time zones? Well we are experiencing it right now, but thankfully my gorgeous, wonderful, thoughtful wife has packed some Earl Grey tea …. thanks Fiona, you little life saver.

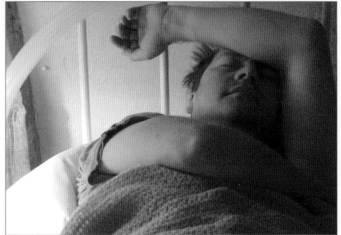

I was going to say that we 'spotted' a little welcoming note from Tony (Reevsie's father in law) containing varying instructions and useful information with advice on what to do and when to do it, on what to see and how to see it etc., but this note, was not terribly welcoming, indeed two pontifications will stick forever in my head.

1. If you hear a knocking at night don't worry (too much) it's just the hornets from the nest outside (my) window trying to get in.
2. Scratch the hob and you're dead!

With merry little reflections of devilish animals the size of a 1980 Nokia cell phone and of gentle reminders not to damage the cooking appliances, I drift off into a wistful, deep and urgent slumber.

Vive le Frog!!!

The bedroom is becoming lighter and as I wake up there are distant sounds of geese being fattened. The truly great thing about shutters is that they don't let any light in. They also keep the Gite safe from naughty or ill intentioned people. The bright blue shutters are everywhere in this farmhouse Everywhere that is except for the window in my adopted bedroom, the window that allows me a millimetre of security from the 1980 Nokia phone that is clearly giving me the big one. Right here, right now. I feel slightly smug knowing that this insidious insect can't get to me, but I shall leave the window closed in any case – at night I'm not so brave.

As I look out from the window my eyes start to digest the splendour of my very own country vista and I wonder what purpose hornets play in the grand scheme of evolution.

It's a crisp late summer morning and Reevsie's up already. Upon opening the kitchen door he has discovered a larger than average truck which one of our continental cousins has deemed necessary to plonk outside the house. Never mind, it is a great back-drop to the photo and I suppose it will add a little contrast.

Chris is snapping away feverishly. He is capturing moods, feels and even spiders' webs.

He has now disappeared by the pool and while I get the tea on (a job I have become accustomed to) I question what he could possibly be doing with his telephoto lens directed at the water. I should have known – there was a frog in the pool. The frog was resting on a stick. A frog on a stick in a pool. This is France after all.

Visions and recipes of frogs' legs mousse come into our heads and deciding that neither would this be a good idea or indeed our serious intention we choose to call the photo – 'The bastard got away' – please enjoy it!

Bergerac market greets us with the ubiquitous hustle and bustle of busy housewives going about their daily shopping and menu planning, and of fabulous food smells, coffee aromas and freshly baked clafoutis that stirs hunger in these English men.

We eat chocolate croissants and drink frothy coffee in a little square before embarking on our major shopping chores! I go to grab my loose change from my back pocket and I find the first of several notes that I had forgotten Fiona had packed for me.

Fiona is a really kind and considerate person. We are not used to being away from each other much and when we are we do things like leave notes for each other.

The note that was in my pocket was to be opened on my first day away. It read
"Give Chris a slap for me"
I did. See photo.

We spotted two lovely, young lady Chefs working in a restaurant nearby. The French shutters were wide open and they were plying their art (actually butterflying sardines) in a small but well equipped open plan kitchen that spills out onto a hidden lane.

Meandering over we chatted with the girls and I asked if my Dad (Reevsie) could take a picture of them. Obligingly they posed and suddenly we had another idea for the front cover of the book. We thanked them and said our goodbyes just as the potato supplier turned up.

Next door to the restaurant a 'calm commotion' was unfolding, involving what seemed to be most of Bergerac's valiant firemen. We couldn't actually see any fires or spot any cats stuck up chimneys but the Brigade were up and down those mechanical ladders like yoyos, noisily shouting instructions to one another.

Tuesday
21ˢᵗ September 2004

Hello Baby,

Hope you arrived safely and had a good journey.
Missing you already
Take Care Babe and have lots of fun it will be worth it!
Give Chris a slap

Love forever
Dahinsky XX

Chris decided that these guys would make superb models in their shiny helmets and pressed blue uniforms and was snapping away happily until the Fire Chief got arsey and asked us to leave the scene.

Upon the realisation that he was dealing with a couple of mute English fools rather than anyone more sinister he allowed us to stay and watch and even struck a macho pose for us.

Walking into the splendid market around the Cathedral we encountered a crowd of shoppers thronging around a man like bees around honey. (The other analogy has something to do with flies). In this case the honey turned out to be an impossibly stereotypical French market vendor. Impossibly typical because I believed his character and general demeanour were almost put on or indeed genuinely fake.

He was wearing the beret; he had the herbs, the crazy handle bar moustache and as for the waffle…

God only knows what old Francois was selling, but it must have been interesting and I wanted to see. He was holding court like a wily magician and by all accounts doing a roaring trade.

This man seemed to spot Reevsie in the distance with his almost devilishly gifted eyesight. Chris was shooting with his telephoto lens but the man bellowed at him to stop taking photos NOW!

CENSORED TO PROTECT THE INNOCENT

PRODUCTEUR
Lot-et-Garonne

Our crafty old mate, we assumed, was the French equivalent of a witch doctor as he was prescribing natural analgesic potions to combat ailments ranging from headaches to gonorrhea (Chris, here's one for you!)

Now having a pretty naff old back – from playing too much rugby as a kid I'm told - and having spent a fortune on unsuccessful Harley Street osteopaths, I decided in my finest French to ask him if he had a treatment for my niggling disc ailments.

Almost before I had finished the question he had pulled up my shirt to reveal the small of my back and cut up the most peculiar looking plant and started to rub the sticky white poison from it on to the affected area of my back.

A few seconds later it happened – the man I had imagined was a witch doctor – was actually the devil. He had given me the most excruciating pain possible on the back of my body. Serious heat, pins and needles and the most violent of reactions possible.

This market is breathtaking. I feel inspired and alive. I adore cooking so much and I love cooking with ingredients that their producers love as much as me. This market offers everything. A million different sausages, a never ending assortment of fruits and berries, vegetables of all descriptions – some that I have never seen. Crusty breads, butters, creams and of course the cheeses.

What I really worship is the difference. Today I am just going to choose some foods. I am going to talk to Reevsie about them. We will take them back to the farm house and cook them. Then we are going to photograph them. Then we are going to write the recipes and edit the pictures. Simple as that. I don't have a schedule. I don't need to rush. I don't have a time to stick to. Actually I don't even know what I'm going to cook. This is great; all we have is enthusiasm and vision. We are both stimulated and remember what it is we love so much about our crafts.

Keeping my shirt up to avoid contact with my burning skin I searched out a café, ran into the toilet and splashed gallons of water over my back. I was literally running around fanning my half naked back and writhing in agony.

Reevsie was running around following me fully dressed and helpless with laughter.

The pain lasted 20 minutes and then vanished as quickly as it had appeared. I guess it did constitute a short term remedy. After all, I had forgotten all about my niggly back pain during that eventful twenty minutes.

We had bought some mussels, some local grapes (should have just stopped and picked them!), some foie gras some fraise de bois – I haven't seen a decent wild strawberry for ages at home. A duck breast, wild mushrooms freshly picked, some salsify - in fact we had bought most of Bergerac Market. I chucked the food in a wooden box and as we walked back to the car guess what? CHRIS FANCIES PIZZA!

As the bloody photographer is threatening a revolution I consider it a prudent move to accept his artistic peculiarities and we slip into a moody, shabby, little bistro to quench our appetites.

Over lunch we talk about our recipes. We want our potential readers to try what they make. It shouldn't matter if mistakes are made along the way. We agree that we definitely don't want the book to be too clinical. We want it to be fun and inspirational. We want it to reflect us, and for it not to be just another boring old cook book.

Chris has suggested that I consider everyone an idiot when writing out the recipes – just so he can under-stand! So from now on he will read each recipe so that even stupid people will know how to follow them! Still, I can't take much of a photo matey.

Moules Á La Mariniére
(Don't be afraid)
Serves:2
(Hungry starters or light snack with a chunk of crusty bread)

Here is what you need

1kg Small mussels –
   washed and scrubbed with "beards" removed
   Dash of olive oil
50ml Dry white wine
1 Small onion – shredded
1 Large carrot – shredded
1 Clove garlic – peeled and crushed
1 Celery stalk – shredded
2 Tablespoons of crème fraiche
   Fresh parsley – ripped
   Salt and pepper
   Knob of butter

What you need to do to it:

1. Wash and scrub mussels, remove "beards" and throw away any that are open.
2. Place a little olive oil in a large pan – heat gently and add mussels.
3. Season with salt and pepper, stir mussels with wooden spoon (because you do!)
4. Add the shredded vegetables and crushed garlic.
5. Add white wine, stir and cover pan.
6. Simmer until the mussels open, add crème fraiche, boil once.
7. Add a knob of butter and ripped parsley and serve.

On the subject of 'stupid' and without wishing to sound condescending it seems to us that there are a good number of stupid people in the world. Some of these stupid people have a lot of splosh. And whilst most rich people are clever we are nevertheless occasionally visited by stupid, rich people. For this reason we would like to create our own brand of foods for people with more money than sense. These fortunate persons, in the enviable position of being able to afford any type of food they yearn for, will become known as THE STUPID MILLIONAIRES (as opposed to the not stupid millionaires).

I take a picture of Reevsie licking his plate, and we have a great idea-if not slightly pervy-of putting a gorgeous girl on the cover licking her plate in ecstasy, yet sort of Carry On Film genre. Even better we can shoot in the restaurant. See the 'gorgeous' Rachel on the cover (like you hadn't noticed!). It is agreed that it should be a book of food, photography and filth.

The chapters should be in simple prose *(that's all you are of capable of, Ed)*, and we have an idea that gorgeous models would grace the titles, pointing at blackboards with schoolmaster's canes in hand. The writing on those boards should be the work of a French national. They have that natural calligraphic ability that is taught to them from early school years.

We should, however not lose sight of the fact that Chris and I are consummate professionals – the food and photos must be the best quality that we can achieve.

We head back to the gite and excitedly take our very first food photos of washing the mussels, then the red mullet.

I will write the recipes as a chef, and Reevsie will read them as a stupid person. If he gets it then anyone can.

Tony & Jane's
Piece of Salmon with armagnac prunes, cabbage & Monbazillac wine
Serves: 2

Thanks to Tony and Jane. We cooked what they left us, including Jane's wonderful armagnac prunes and muscat grapes picked from their vine!

Here is what you need

2x   Pieces of salmon, approx 80g each

1x   Curly cabbage

8x   Prunes (marinated in armagnac)

8x   Black olives – chopped

8x   Langoustine tails

      Walnut oil (approx 30-50ml)

      Monbazillac wine (approx 50ml)

1x   Tablespoon crème fraiche

      Approx 50g unsalted butter – cubed

      Handful seedless grapes (I used Muscat)

      Salt and Pepper

      A little flour

What you need to do to it:

1. Shred the cabbage and plunge into boiling salted water (2 minutes). Strain and allow to cool.

2. Chop prunes and olives, mix into a bowl with cabbage, season with salt and pepper and bind with a little walnut oil.

3. Gently coat salmon and langoustine tails in flour (seasoned with salt and pepper).

4. Add a little walnut oil to a shallow pan and fry salmon turning once approx 4 – 6 minutes, then fry langoustine tails in the same way, 2 - 3 minutes turning once.

5. Add wine to a pan over direct heat and allow to reduce by half.

6. Add crème fraiche, boil once, whisk in cubed butter, don't allow to boil again (or it will solidify).

7. Throw grapes into butter sauce, adjust seasoning and serve.

8. Dress cabbage, salmon and langoustine as in picture.

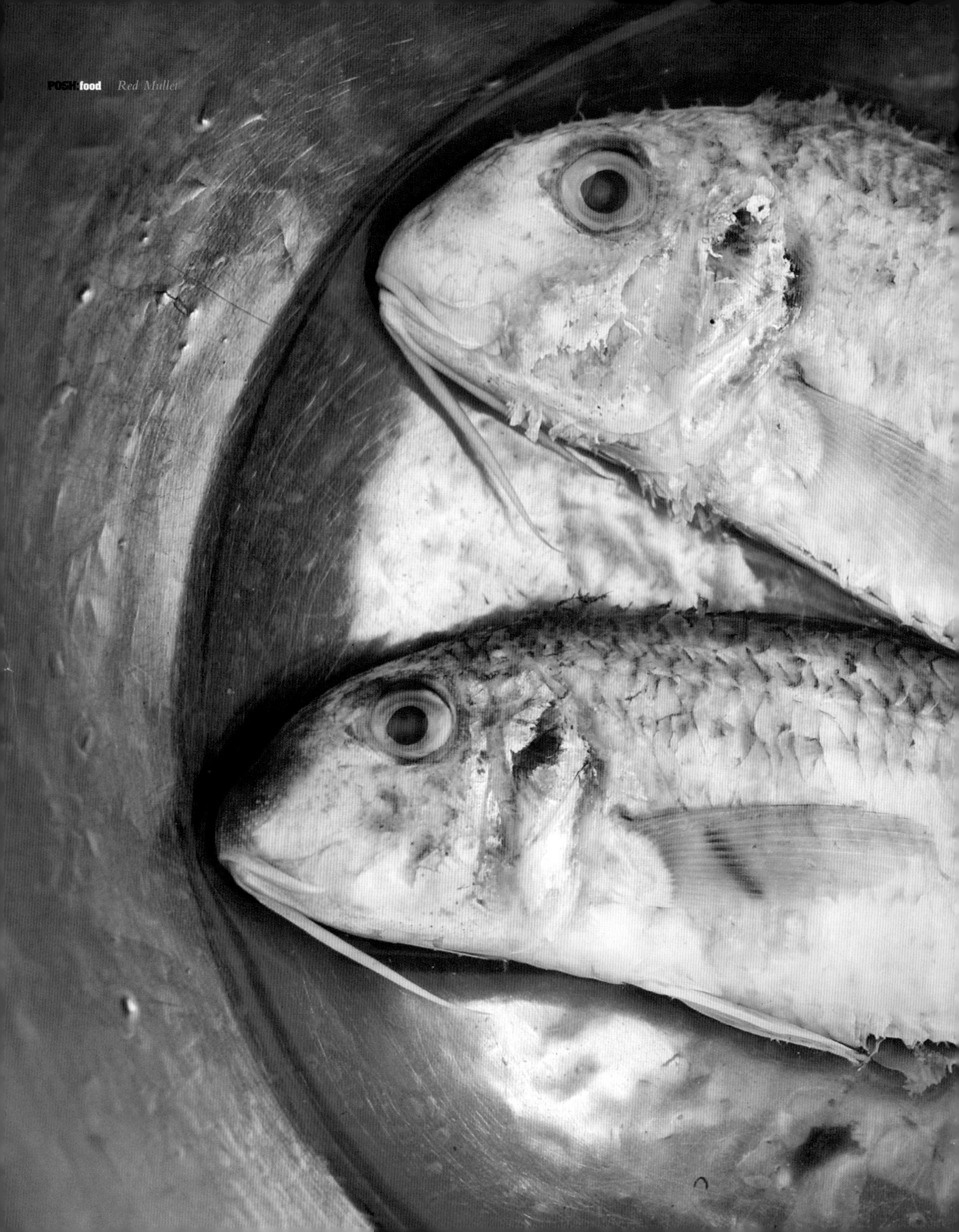

Red Mullet

Day 55

Red Mullet can be bought scaled and 'Pin Boned'

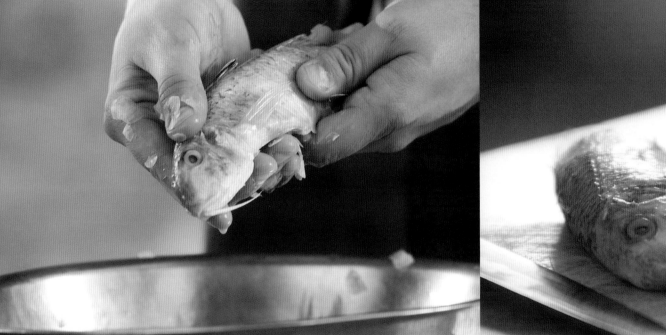

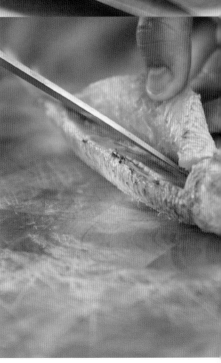

For your help:

1: Wash the scales off under cold
    running water.

2: Cut off the fins.

3: Place the knife along the back
    bone, starting near the head.

4: Lift off the fillets and take out
    the pin bones with tweezers.

but I'm going to show off because I am a Chef!

Red Herring

Please note: The "Bikini Heaven 2004" belongs to Reevsie!

Grilled Fillet of Red Mullet with Jalapeno Pesto
Serves: 2

What you need:

2x   Fillets of Red Mullet (80g) bones removed *(previous page, pay attention!)*

2x   Baby Carrots – sliced

6x   Baby Red Radishes – sliced

1x   Celery Stick – sliced

1x   Handful haricot Green Beans

6x   Sliced Jalapeno Peppers

6x   Extra Fine Cornichons

1x   Spring Onion – diced

     Salt & Pepper

     Virgin Olive Oil

     Pinch of Chilli Flakes

     Flour to coat fish

What you need to do to it:

1. Blanch beans in boiling salted water until just hard. Allow to cool then peel.

2. Heat a little olive oil in shallow pan - 'introduce'. chopped carrots and celery just to soften slightly.

3. In a bowl, mix beans, celery, carrots, shredded spring onion, jalapenos and radishes.

4. Bind with olive oil, add chilli flakes and season with salt and pepper.

5. Heat olive oil in a pan, roll skin side of red mullet in seasoned flour.

6. 'Seal' red mullet skin side down for 1 minute.

7. Turn over, cook for a further 2 minutes.

8. Lay across market vegetables and serve.

To be enjoyed with light reading

Tony and Jane recount a wonderful story concerning their builders on an earlier trip out to the Gite.

The old boys, not knowing that Tony and Jane were home at that particular time, suddenly spotted Tony coming out of the back door for an early morning dip.

"Attention, attention!", shouted the builder, and whilst struggling to understand what was going on or what the old chap was saying, Tony suddenly heard the loud rantings of "Dynamite, dynamite" and he rapidly withdrew back into the farmhouse, slamming the shutters behind him.

Bang! Boom! Bang!

The dynamite exploded in his front garden! These two great characters had found a conveniently labour saving way to destroy some boulders that were deemed too large to break up manually.

This is France after all.

Amongst other things I have decided to make some fairly typical French pancakes, with a less than typical Wild Fruit and Gin Sugar sauce. Unfortunately we had forgotten to buy some of the essentials and Reevsie had kindly offered to go shopping whilst I continued preparing foods for the next photographs.

On his way to the shop in Beaumont, Chris came across an enormous chicken sitting in the middle of an otherwise un passable road.

Beeping the horn of the monster truck was a fruitless exercise, as the suicidal chicken refused to move. Chris got out of the truck and waving his arms about frantically attempted to shoo it away.

The fowl once more refused to budge.

Chris then decided to give it a gentle kick, by now desperate to get on his way.

The chicken retorted with a bite to his foot. This was becoming a man thing – a stand off!

Reevsie looked around and realizing that nobody was about he attempted to drop kick the bird.

Jonny Wilkinson eat your heart out.

Summer Fruits and Gin Sauce
Serves:10-12

Here is what you need

100g small sweet strawberries (wild!)
100g blueberries
100g forest strawberries
100g raspberries
100g redcurrants
100ml water
150g caster sugar
50ml – ish of gin – we used more-ish!

Simply:

1. Boil the sugar and water in a pan until it starts to change colour – careful it's hot!

2. Prepare the fruit (hull the strawberries and rinse all, place in a heat proof bowl). When a light coloured caramel has been achieved pour over the fruit then pour in the gin and allow to cool.

3. Serve hot or cold with pancakes.

Crepe Mix
Serves:10-12

Here is what you need:

100g Plain flour
2x Medium free range eggs
Approx 200ml milk
80g Caster sugar
Knob of unsalted butter

What you need to do to it:

1. Whisk the eggs together.
2. Add the flour, then sugar then beat.
3. Slowly add the milk, little by little until the required consistency is achieved (because of egg size differences etc. it is difficult to be precise with how much milk is needed, but the batter should just coat the back of your wooden spoon).
4. Place a knob of butter in a pancake pan, ladle a little batter in the sizzling butter and turn over after a couple of minutes. Cook until evenly browned.
5. Dress with the fruits in gin and dredge with icing sugar.

Many people put salt in their pancake batter – I have never known or asked why – so I don't!!

(and look at them!!)

He was doing fine at the shop and knowing the French language quite well I had explained to him that beurre was butter, lait was milk etc, and that if he had any problems he should give me a call to translate our requirements.

He did phone with just one question. He couldn't find the flour and would need to ask the assistant for it.

"Farine" I said. "but we shall need the special strong flour, the one that is called "baise mon cul."

Sheepishly Reevsie returned to the Gite, with a bag full of ingredients, strong flour and a ruddy complexion. I shall leave you to look up the translation.

Sorry Reevsie.

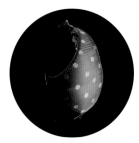

SMARTY PANT

"Baise mon cul!"

It's 7.45 in the evening on our second day. We've had another great day of cooking and shooting and we are both more enthusiastic than ever. I have just finished the latest pile of washing up and Chris, who is in the process of editing millions of photos, has come into the kitchen.

He opens the fridge.
"Anything to eat, matey?"
"Not really buddy, but we could try that nice looking creperie up the road"

The rustic little dining room in a rustic little house can be found down one of those leafy country lanes that are abundant in this region. The existence of this particular eatery is only known to us because of a sign on the side of the road 'Open for food between Tuesday and Sunday – at meal times.'

Well it's now 8pm on Wednesday. The Restaurant is shut. Naturellement, this is France after all.

Pushing on to Cadouin (home of Reevsie's mediaeval dancing girl) we discover a superb pizza restaurant. It's an intimate little affair with very hospitable owners who even speak blighty. We have since come to use this Restaurant time and time again and have befriended 'mine host'. We promise ourselves to include this pizzeria in the book and munch our way through our very garlicky starters (should freshen Reevsie's breath up a bit).

One word of advice here. If ordering the beautiful, fresh spaghetti Carbonara, the pasta will arrive with a raw egg yolk in the shell right in the middle of the dish. Now I prefer to eat my eggs cooked, and after what Chris did to that poor chicken earlier, there's no way I'm eating that!

To make **creamed salsify** simply peel six fingers of salsify, boil in milk until soft, strain, season, add crème fraiche and mash up.

Our foolish dinner confabulations and ideas are brimming with endless possibilities. We banter about a page of Oscar winners – for people we ironically want to thank for helping make the book possible. We talk about the battle of the cheeses. My particular favourite is 'Stinking Bishop' a pre-eminent cheese from our own shores, versus something typically French like Camembert or Brie. We shall have to wait and see whether these ideas will turn up in the book. We ponder names for the book, names like 'Tarts, truffles and tantrums', or 'Day tossers, no trippers', 'Pigs in shit' and many, many more.

It's Tuesday – I've just finished cooking duck with creamed salsify. I'm pleased with the results and delighted with Reevsie's photos. We think that each recipe should have a cook's or photographer's tip to accompany it.

The tip for this one should read something like this: when preparing salsify it is important to peel it by the edge of a warm swimming pool, next to a pretty Gite down in the Dordogne.

I know Chris is an arty type of bloke and over time I have learnt not to ask questions of his addictive and continual snappings. Indeed I have experienced his bewildering results. This time he is taking photos of what seems to be a fairly normal sort of garden wall - lots and lots of photos.

Mark *"Why have we travelled half way round France to take pictures of an outside wall?"* Chris *"Fuck off!"*

'Nough said.

Duck with bacon, girolles and foie gras
Serves:1 fat photographer or 2

What you need:

2x   Duck breast (200g each)

2x   Small potatoes (balled with a melon baller)

1x   Handful of fresh girolle mushrooms – ripped

2x   Small shallots – sliced

3x   Cloves of garlic – smashed

2x   Slices foie gras

100g Bacon lardons

50ml Red wine

40ml Beef stock

      Olive oil

      Maldon sea salt

What you need to do to it:

1. Boil the balled potatoes in a little salted water, then strain and leave.
2. Trim the duck breast and score fat.
3. Heat a frying pan.
4. Season the duck and place skin side down in the hot fry pan (no oil is necessary as the duck is pretty fatty).
5. Leave until brown (3-4 minutes).
6.. Turn over and continue cooking in the pan for another couple of minutes and place in oven (fan assisted 220°C/Gas mark 7) for 6 minutes (medium).
7. Bring out and allow to rest.

Meanwhile, make the sauce

1. Splash a little olive oil in a fry pan – heat and sauté bacon, when brown add the sliced shallots, then ripped girolle mushrooms.
2. Next add the potatoes, season and stir a little.
3. Add red wine and allow to reduce almost all the way.
4. Add the beef stock and boil once.
5. Spoon the sauce onto a plate and place the duck (which can be sliced) over the top.
6. Place a piece of seasoned foie gras on top of the duck and serve.

I used a little creamed salsify as well (because I'm like that!). To make it simply peel six fingers of salsify, boil in milk until soft, strain, season add crème fraiche and mash up.

A couple of months ago I bought a new phone and I'm not much good with technology. It's a picture phone and I'm really pleased with it. I purchased it so that I can share experiences and good times with Fiona and the girls, but all I seem to receive are rude images. Still they are great fun, and much easier than texting to keep in touch. It was therefore lovely to get a message from my other boys and girls who were busy looking after my Restaurant in Essex. At the time they were together at one of our weekly staff meetings when the message appeared on my phone. "Miss you." "Yeah right." and guess what, "I don't miss you guys one little bit!"

Anyway, for some reason my phone has turned itself off and I can't get it back on. Even Captain Big Bladder (who rates himself as a bit of a techno king) has given up. We have now tried every button and there's nothing left for it. I shall have to borrow his phone to ring my wife to find out how to turn the bloody thing back on. How embarrassing, how un-manly!

It's Friday. It's chucking it down with rain and we need sunshine for some outside shots today. It doesn't really matter as the rain clears so quickly here. The sun will shine through soon and dry the land efficiently.

Meanwhile, we make the most of our time and head off to a well stocked vegetarian nightmare - the Butcher's shop nestling on the corner in the small town called Beaumont.

The Butcher's wife is corpulent and fleshy – and so she should be. Who ever heard of a thin Butcher's wife? Chefs must also be fat. Never trust a thin Cook! Photographers on the other hand have no excuse! Here we buy some lamb, a fillet of well hung beef – not quite my usual Aberdeen Angus, but pretty good - and some buttery and beautifully tender veal.

The butcher assures us that the weather will improve shortly and with these good tidings we head to a coffee bar to join the folk reminiscent of the village people. The coffee is too strong and we both feel sick.

I always find it interesting that the French have such wonderful produce and that they are allowed to openly display it in their shops. We must have different germs in the U.K. as we would never get away with hanging the meats, sausages, game and hams in the assiduous way that they do. At home, a cheese can't be out of the fridge to ripen for more than a couple of minutes before some bureaucrat jumps down your neck. Generally that same bureaucrat has taken their lead from Belgium.
The French people generally live longer than us. Well done, a hint here perhaps!

Today I want to make a really good olive oil mashed potato to go with roast chicken and peas. I've forgotten my ricer so we pop into an Aladdin's cave of a shop which sells absolutely every thing from shotguns and rifles to baby toys. We find the ricer and some really alarming bright orange baseball caps. These caps are seriously shitty. I mean 100 percent nylon and loud as you like.

We are going to wear these hats when we go to the airport to collect our wives – they're due to come over tomorrow night. We have an idea to present an orange hat to anybody that helps in the making of our book and consider running some sort of competition in the book with the top prize being one of these horrific limited edition hats. The prize hat would of course be signed by the authors and would probably fetch a pound or two on eBay! We pay the lady for the ricer and six hats. The shopkeeper thinks we are demented. We are English after all.

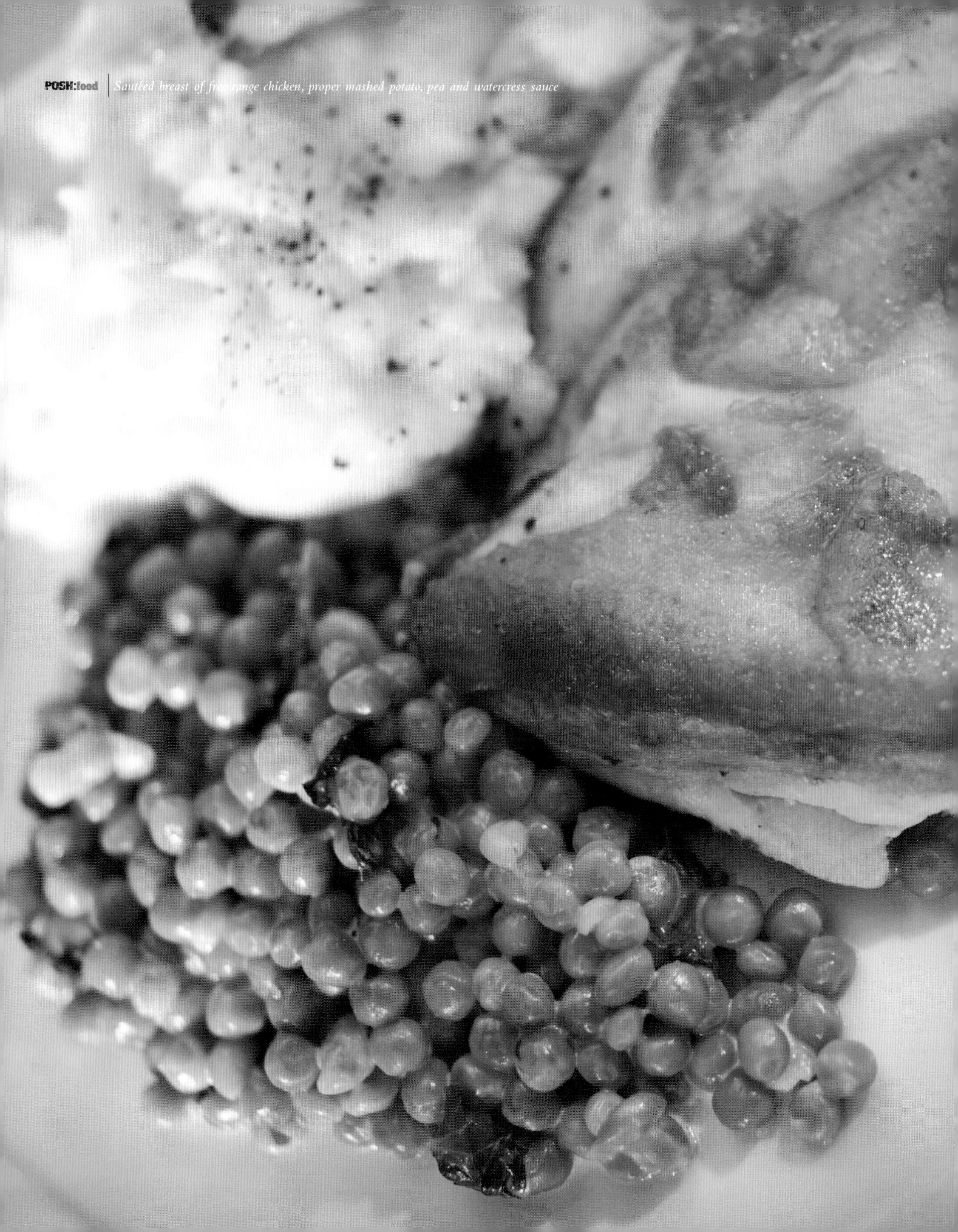

Sautéed breast of free range chicken, proper mashed potato, pea and watercress sauce
Serves: 2

Here is what you need:

2x   Breast of free range chicken (I used corn-fed)

1x   Bunch watercress leaves

200g Petit pois (extra fine in a jar)

1x   Dollop crème fraiche

4x   Large potatoes

       Butter

       Pinch of fresh grated nutmeg

       Chicken stock

       Olive oil

       Salt and Pepper

       Flour

Make Mashed Potato:

1. Peel and chop the spuds, boil in a pan with enough chicken stock to cover.

2. When soft, strain (keep any chicken stock for vegetarian soup!)

3.. Return to the pan, dry, pass through a spud masher and season with salt, pepper, olive oil, nutmeg and crème fraiche – keep until needed.

Everything else:

1. Season chickens with salt and pepper and rub skin side in a little flour, pat off any excess.

2. Heat olive oil in a pan and seal the chicken (skin side down) until it starts to brown.

3. Turn over and place in a hottish oven (200°C fan assisted/Gas mark 6) for approx 15 minutes.

4. Heat the petits pois in a tiny bit of their juice and rip some watercress.

5. When the peas have boiled, add the watercress leaves, a dollop of crème fraiche and a knob of butter – no seasoning necessary.

6. Allow the chicken to rest and arrange on a white plate.

NB: I was going to shell fresh peas – but honestly just buy the best French petits pois in a jar and taste the flavour.

The weather is already brightening and wearing our new fashion accessories we head on to a market in Cadouin le Buisson. Our attention is immediately drawn to a hairdressing salon. Nothing really funny about the name on the sign above 'fanny coiffure', but bearing in mind coiffure is French for hairdresser it does beg a question. I pose under the sign like a silly school boy watched with a perplexed glare by a Gallic brother.

Among all the fine foods Reevsie manages to take a great photo of a market trader smoking a cigarette. He names the photo 'Hag with a fag' – I hope he chooses to feature this one somewhere in the book.

A familiar smell is wafting across our noses and it is coming from the pizzas being freshly baked in a mobile market stall a few yards away. The man in control is none other that 'mine host' from the pizzeria restaurant we have come to love. Eagerly he offers his hand, slightly coated in flour and he has some excellent news for us.

We had been talking to him about truffles, and were looking for someone who hunts for them with a pig in the traditional way. His wife has spoken to a woman who knows a man who has a friend who still searches out this black gold in the customary and time honoured fashion.

We decide that we should return to this area in the truffle season and Reevsie suggests that somewhere in the book we should capture pictures of ourselves at work in our own businesses – to provide evidence that we are actually professional people and not just good for nothing layabouts. We also consider a chapter named 'The dogs of the Dordogne' as there are just so many handsome specimens etched in the digital memory of the photographer's Kodak.

If I had to choose a picture of myself it would be one that Chris took some years ago. It's the one of me in my Chef's whites, leaning back in a chair on a summer's day – with a good bottle of plonk (see following page). The picture is entitled 'pissed', and has found a home at my restaurant, as well as in the toilet of my Mum and Dad's house (don't tell Reevsie).

The fat butcher's wife was right. The afternoon has cleared up and we spend another special day creating, cooking, shooting and laughing.

CENSORED TO PROTECT THE INNOCENT

'Pissed.'

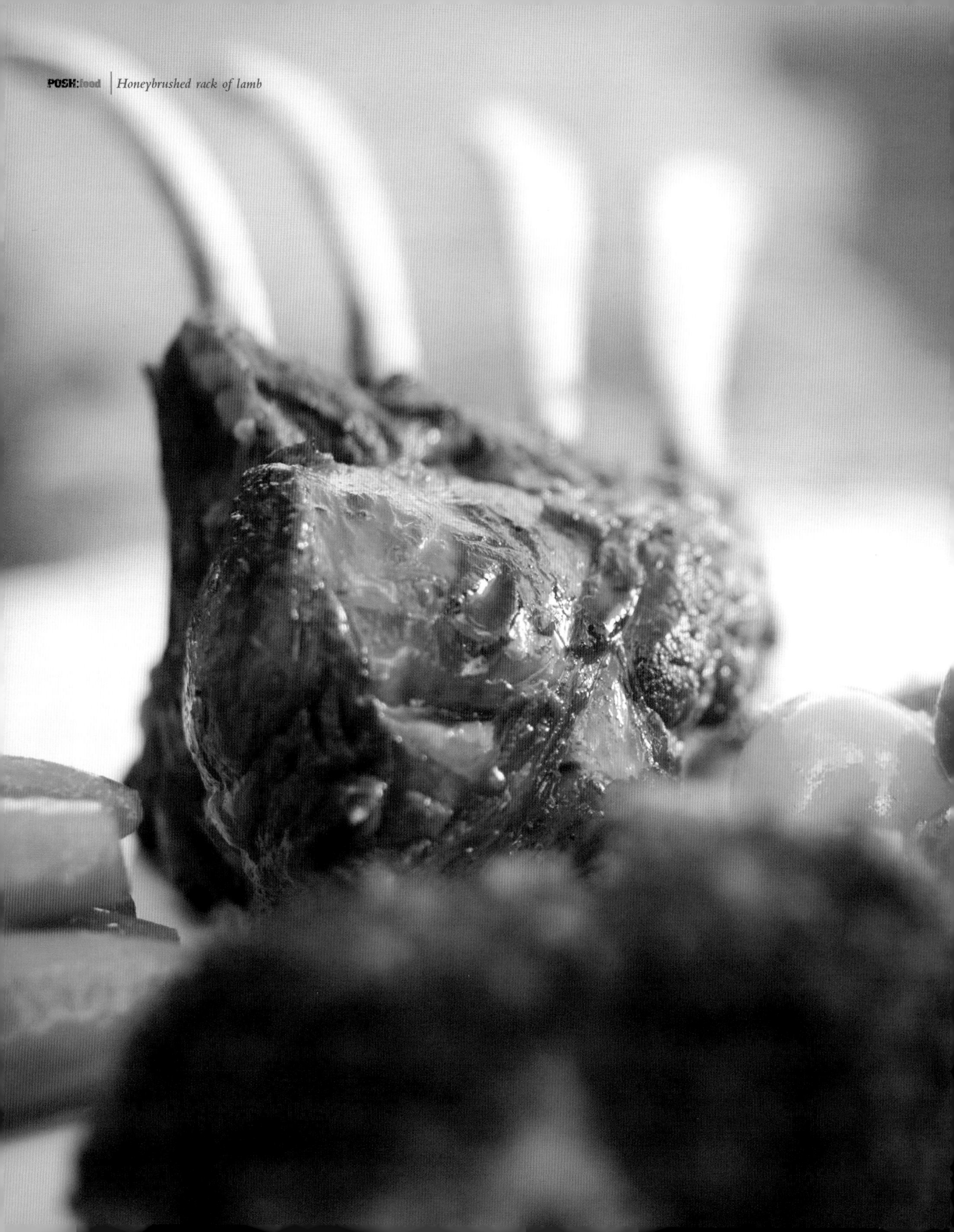

Honeybrushed Rack (or chump) of Lamb
Serves:2

Here is what you need:

1x   8 bone rack of lamb or

2x   4 bone rack or

2x   Small chump (approx 200g each)

20x Red baby tomatoes

20x Green baby tomatoes

10x Yellow pear tomatoes

4x   Pieces of broccoli

2x   Carrots (large) nicely cut

     Salt and pepper

     Butter

     Cooking oil and olive oil

     A little caster sugar

1x   Tablespoon runny honey

     Knob of butter

What you need to do to it:

1. Season the lamb with salt and pepper.
2. In a pan melt a knob of butter and splash of cooking oil.
3. Seal the lamb (both sides) until nicely brown.
4. (If using rack of lamb it is now important to put foil on the bones to prevent them from burning in the oven).
5. Place lamb in a hot oven (220°C fan assisted/Gas mark 7) for 15-20 minutes (medium).
6. Cook the carrots in a little water, caster sugar and knob of butter.
7. Plunge the broccoli into boiling salted water until tender.
8. Warm a pan and roll the tomatoes in good olive oil, but don't allow to get too hot or they'll mash!
9. Remove the lamb and allow to rest for a good 5 minutes.
10. Brush the lamb with runny honey (on the skin).
11. Warm the other ingredients and serve.

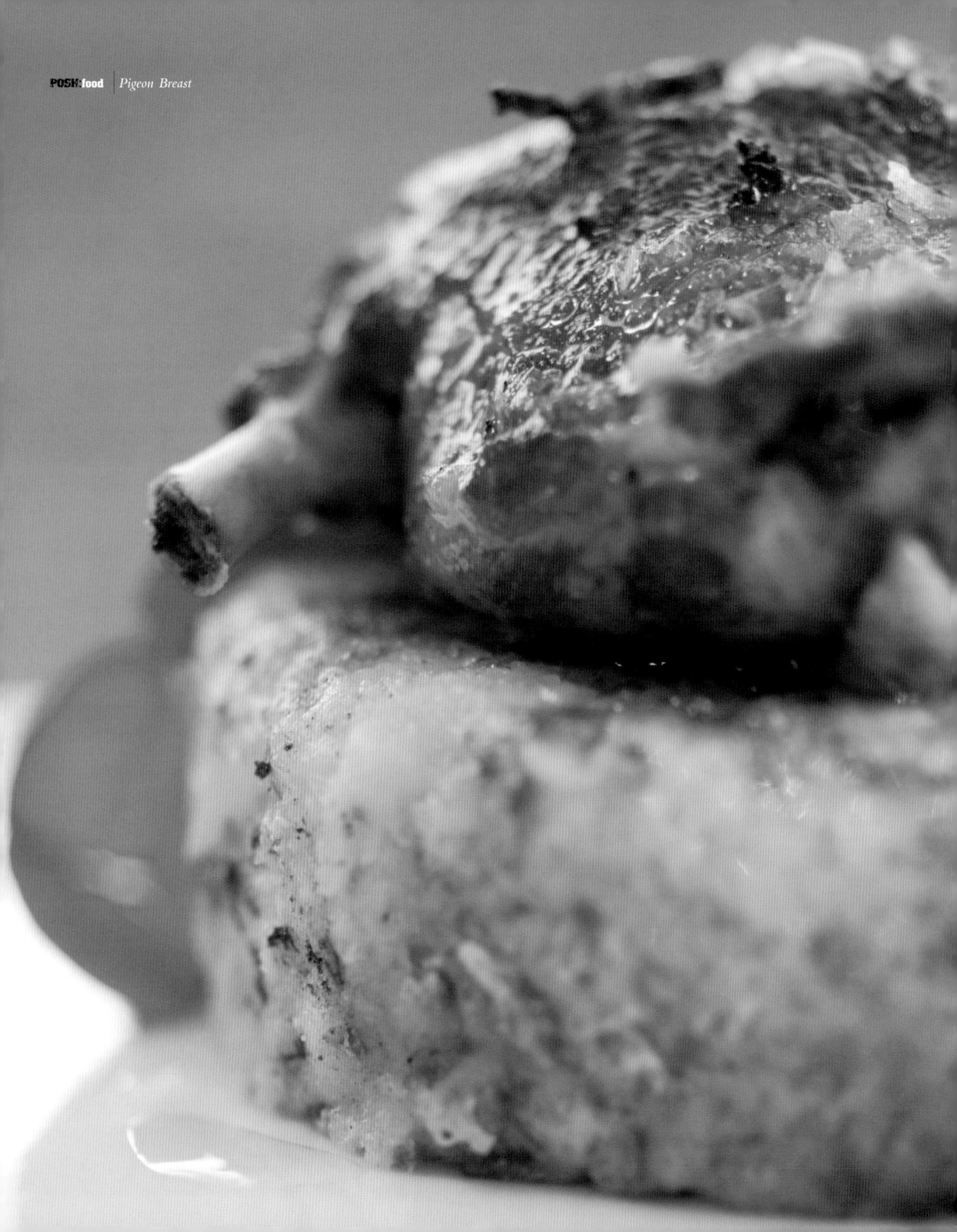

Here is what you need:

4x   Pigeon breasts

250g Brussels sprouts

2x   Large potatoes

250g Haricots cuisines (butter beans in goose fat)

1x   Bunch fresh watercress leaves (to garnish)

1x   Small onion

4x   Cloves crushed garlic

     Splash of Worcestershire sauce

     Salt and pepper

     Olive oil

     A little flour

     Vegetable stock

     A 'dollop' of crème fraiche

What you need to do to it:

1. Peel and boil carrots in enough chicken stock to cover.
2. Purée carrots, add a dollop of crème fraiche and set aside.
3. Boil spuds in salted water, when soft dry well and break up.
4. Shred brussels sprouts and plunge into boiling salted water to soften (3 minutes). Then strain.
5. Sauté onion in a little olive oil.
6. Mix onions, potatoes, salt and pepper, brussels sprouts and a dash of Worcester sauce together.
7. Mould into little 'round patties' and pat in flour, then gently fry.
8. Heat oil in a pan – season pigeon breasts, then fry skin down until just brown.
9. Turn over and continue cooking on the other side.
10. Place in hot oven (220°C fan assisted/Gas mark 7) for 3-4 minutes.
11. Heat the posh baked beans.
12. Take out pigeon, allow to rest and dress on plate with carrot purée, bubble and squeak etc – as in photo.

Pan fried Pigeon Breasts with brussels sprout bubble and squeak and posh baked beans

Serves: 2

Pork Tenderloin, calvados apples and a 'sort of' Mustard Buerre Blanc
Serves:2

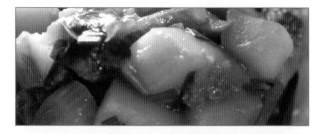

Here is what you need:

1x   Piece tenderloin of pork (350g)

2x   Red apples – chopped

2x   Shallots – diced

50ml Calvados

3x   Plums – chopped

1x   Tablespoon caster sugar

  Cooking oil and olive oil

  Butter

  Salt and pepper

Mustard Buerre Blanc

50ml White wine vinegar

1x   Tablespoon crème fraiche (or double cream)

75g Unsalted butter – cut into cubes

1x   Teaspoon coarse grain mustard

1x   Teaspoon chopped fresh chives

What you need to do to it:

1.   Heat pan with a splash of olive oil.
2.   Gently sauté the diced shallots and chopped apples.
3.   Add chopped plums and the sugar and allow to caramelise for a minute.
4.   Add the calvados and season with salt and pepper.
5.   "Stew" until most of the calvados has been absorbed but the apples still have 'le crunch'.
6.   Season the pork with salt and pepper and seal in a hot oiled pan until all sides are nicely browned.
7.   Place in a hot oven (220°C fan assisted/Gas mark 7) for about 20 minutes or until firm to touch.
8.   Take out meat and rest it for 5–8 min.
9.   Make the Buerre Blanc.
10.   Heat the white wine vinegar in a pot and allow to reduce by half.
11.   Reduce heat and add the crème fraiche.
12.   Add mustard.
13.   Whisk in butter, season with pepper and throw in chives.
14.   Dress together on a plate with roast or mashed potatoes.

Tip: if you want to make certain your meat is cooked insert a skewer into the thickest part, pull it on your bottom lip and if it burns - the meat is cooked!

Complicated Cutlet of Veal with green and yellow beans
Serves: 2

Here is what you need:

2x Veal cutlets

Approx 75g green beans

Approx 75g yellow (butter) beans

3x Large potatoes

1x Large leek

16 Small shallots

Cooking Oil

Salt and Pepper

Butter

What you need to do to it:

1. Place the shallots in an oven proof dish, splash with olive oil and roast in their skins in an oven (180°C fan assisted/Gas mark 4) for about 20 minutes.

2. Top and tail the beans and blanch in boiling salted water, then cool in iced water and save.

3. Peel the spuds, grate, season and dry out in a clean cloth – squeezing lots of liquid out.

4. Heat a non-stick pan with a little cooking oil and make a rosti with the grated spud – yes you can! (Or just serve new potatoes).

5. Salt and pepper the veal cutlets, heat another pan and seal the veal on both sides (nice and brown).

6. Place in a hot oven (220°C fan assisted/Gas mark 7) – where it will remain for about 15 minutes (medium).

7. Meanwhile, roughly chop the leek, plunge into boiling salted water, drain and bind with a little olive oil and salt and pepper.

8. Take out the veal, allow to rest. Warm through all the other ingredients and dress the plate.

Whole, roasted shallots are really tasty. When slightly cold, squeeze out the middle.

The Ultimate Tomato Ketchup

Here is what you need:

6x   Plum Tomatoes (blanched in boiling water to remove skin and roughly chopped)

1x   Big bunch of fresh basil – ripped

1x   Tablespoon fresh thyme

1x   Onion – roughly chopped

1x   Head garlic – smashed

4x   Small pickled red chilli peppers – chopped

100ml White wine

50ml Balsamic vinegar

50g   Brown sugar

1x   Teaspoon of chilli flakes

      Olive oil

      Splash of Tabasco

What you need to do to it:

1. Heat a little olive oil in a pan.
2. Add roughly chopped onions and sweat.
3. Add crushed garlic and chopped tomatoes and turn down heat.
4. Add chopped chilli pepper, chilli flakes and a splash of Tabasco.
5. Add white wine and balsamic vinegar.
6. Add sugar and season with salt and pepper.
7. Turn down the heat and simmer as gently as possible for as long as possible until nearly all the liquid is reduced.
8. Add the thyme and ripped basil.
9. The flavour will burst out – the sauce should still be a little "chunky".
10. Finally, add a splash of olive oil.

Serve with the Ultimate Steak and Chips.

NOTE: Many recipes will have you adding tomato paste – why?

The Ultimate Waitress
if only we were sober!!!

The Ultimate Happy Shopper

buying food from Monpazier Market.

You can't go to the Dordogne without sampling the best Foie Gras in the world.

While at Monpazier market we brought a slab of the 'local delicacy', which would have cost a fortune at home. No recipe needed – just eat it with crusty French bread and cornichons.

P.S. It's Rachel's all time favourite, but this is OUR LUNCH SO BUY YOUR OWN!

Cep and Girolle Soup
Serves:2

Here is what you need:

100g Fresh girolles – washed

100g Fresh cêpes – washed

2x Shallots

4x Cloves of garlic – smashed

3x Tablespoons crème fraiche (optional)

1x Medium potato – chopped roughly

Chicken stock (or vegetable stock to keep them happy!)

Salt and fresh ground black pepper

Ripped parsley and basil

It's as simple as this:

1. Rip the girolles and cêps.

2. Slice the shallots.

3. Roughly cut the potatoes.

4. Smash the garlic.

5. Sauté all the above in a little olive oil in a pan.

6. Season with salt and pepper.

7. Cover with stock and simmer until spuds are soft.

8. Spoon in crème fraiche and a few herbs.

9. This soup can then be blended – but we chose to leave it lumpy and served with pain de campagne (Bread! Stupid!).

It's early morning Saturday – the day our wives arrive. It's a bright crisp sunny morning and we decide to visit the market in Villeréal. Now this market seems to be more of a local market for local people. I think most of the traders here have had a late night with too much Pernod, as they seem to be a bit grumpy and it's clear that they don't like foreigners (well us) too much. I get like this when I consume too much cheese and port late in the evening.

I was about to take a picture of a rotisserie of thirty chickens cooking perfectly and smelling divine when the fowl trader became vociferous with me. Obviously he didn't want his produce photographed. I bowed out gracefully, apologised and surmised that he must have considered me to be a member of the notorious chicken police. Still, your loss Monsieur, once we sell a million copies of this book, you will be desolé.

We did come across a decent bloke, however. He was the one that sold us a fine, buttery, flaky, warm Armagnac tart. He actually sprayed it with one of those water dispensers that gardeners use to kill greenfly on roses – just hope he washed it out first! It turns out he often visits England and with the frequency of Ryanair flights, we wonder if it would be possible to start importing his delicious patisserie tarts?

We find two other things of beauty. One is the huge tub of crème fraiche which is perfect for all cooking purposes. It is a thick cream, treated with a culture that makes it slightly acidic, but not sour. Still annoyed with the attitude of the chicken seller I ponder the thought that these three words can be associated with France, 'culture, sour and acidic.'

Indeed this is a country of many contrasts.

The other thing of beauty is the large pair of polyester type pants that are hanging from the rag vendor's market stall. They are pretty horrible but nevertheless have attracted a good deal of interest from some older French Mesdames. Once again I am obliged to pose by these pants for the sake of Chris's art.

Thankfully I have managed to prevent Chris from buying a pair for his wife!

This has nothing to do with anything, but as an arty farty photograph, this is a lovely example of making the mundane look nearly interesting (*can anyone see a robot face with piercings?*).

With a truckload of food we once again drive back to the farm house. The conversation has reverted to the name of the book. We have ditched the 'Tarts, truffles and tantrums' idea – far too Elton John.

I am really happy with the food I cooked today, and of course with the photographs. I did have my first cock-up though, and regrettably it did cause me to go into a bit of a tantrum.

The cock-up occurred with the profiteroles. The oven was too hot and they went crispy without rising properly. I swore a bit and made another batch and placed them into the oven – which was now set at the proper temperature.

Gathering up the first bunch of mishaps I went out to the truck and pulled out my trusted 7 iron. (Never lets me down, always gets me out of trouble.) I placed the mishaps in a pile on the ground and started to swing, remembering what the pro always told me. "Slowly back, say to yourself 'Tiiiiiiiiiiger Woooooooods. At the top of the swing pull down, pull the trigger and watch the ball.' (Or in this case a badly risen profiterole.) I must have been getting sixty yards out of those profiteroles and turning around I heard the ever present clicking of my chum's camera. I am not that happy with my swing at the moment. Not happy that is until I watch Chrissy boy's masterful stroke.

I forget the next bunch of profiteroles and they are burnt too.

Profiteroles with custard, dark and white chocolate sauce
Makes:20/25

Here is what you need:

50ml	Water
50ml	Milk
70g	Unsalted butter
100g	Plain flour
2-3	Eggs (depending on size) – beaten

What you need to do to it:

1. Beat eggs in a bowl.
2. Put water, milk and butter in a pan and heat gently until the butter has melted.
3. Remove from heat and add flour (in one go) and beat madly.
4. Continue beating until it forms a thick paste that holds together and comes away from the sides of the pan.
5. Transfer to a clean bowl, cool for a few minutes then gradually add the beaten egg a little at a time to form a really smooth paste – judge the amount of egg needed – the mix should pipe well but not be runny.
6. Cool.
7. Line a baking tray with parchment and preheat the oven to 180°C fan assisted/Gas mark 4.
   Make sure the oven is up to temperature.
8. Pipe out the choux balls (10p size) but leave enough room on the tray for them to grow.
9. Bake for about 20 minutes or until brown and cool on a wire rack.

Custard Filling:

300ml Milk

3x Egg whites

50g Caster sugar

2x Tablespoons plain flour

2x Teaspoons cornflour

What you need to do to it:

1. Beat the egg yolks, sugar and flour in a bowl.
2. Place milk in a saucepan and boil.
3. Mix the hot milk into the egg mix.
4. Bring to the boil stirring madly (if you stop, the custard will split).
5. Cool and save ready to fill the profiteroles.

Dark Chocolate Sauce:

100g Dark chocolate

100ml Crème fraiche

White Chocolate Sauce:

100g White chocolate

100ml Crème fraiche

What you need to do to it:

1. Warm the cream in a milk pan.
2. Smash the chocolate and mix into the warm cream.

There is just time for a quick dip, a cold beer and a kitchen clean up before collecting the girls from the airport, following their early evening flight.

Incredibly the hob has remained damage free and has scrubbed up as good as new. I have a kind of warm and smug inner feeling now, knowing that Tony can't kill me for scratching his beloved appliance.

We think it would be really funny to wear our horrible redneck, orange hats when we meet the girls and upon arrival at the airport's tiny bar we seem to have scared all the young children. We buy a beer for me (I'm not driving) and a coffee for Chris. The barmaid is only too happy to take a photo of the two of us.

Waiting for the 9pm to arrive from Stansted we take up a comfortable position on the perimeter fence looking very much like Dumb and Dumber.

Following a screech of brakes the girls exit the aircraft and start walking towards us across the tarmac. They thought that we were a couple of touched baggage handlers until Chris flashed his light. It then dawned on these poor, embarrassed things that, yes we were their husbands.

Keeping her head down Fiona said to Rachel "Don't look – they are ours!" "Charming" I thought, especially as we had taken the trouble to bring their new orange hats with us.

We drove straight down to our well frequented pizza restaurant and although it took 35 minutes to get there the girls didn't stop moaning all the way. Having had a couple of cold beers, I found the journey quite amusing, but I decided to side with the girls and started my own little moans about the duration of our travel and the poor calibre of Reevsie's driving.

We murder a scrummy meal with our soul mates and frantically catch up on the news that we hadn't realised was occurring. A few days without telly, just a time of uninterrupted, culinary, photographic, self induced solitude.

It's around midnight and we make our way back to the Gite. I can see that Reevsie's getting a little fed up with the continual moaning from the girls. To be fair his driving is crap. He blames it on my "Bloody Tonka Toy suspension". Who does he think he is? Bloody MG driver, bloody hairdresser's car anyway!

Back at base camp Fiona has a surprise for us. She has made a broken chocolate biscuit cake. A broken chocolate biscuit cake and a cup of Earl Grey Rosie Lee.

Sunday Morning

The girls flatly refuse to get up at our normal 6.30am time. (In fact it was usually closer to 8am, but we didn't tell them that.) Eventually we all surface, and after I refuse to make any breakfast we go out for the day. I don't want my clean kitchen to get dirty again.

Our easy pace brought us to another stunning market in a town that calls itself Issigeac and we are fortunate enough to bump into a charming and dandy man who is selling Perigord truffles. Monsieur Martin turns out to be the major 'truffeculteur' of the entire area. There are really only two areas in the world that are famed for their truffles. One is in the North of Italy (home of the fabulous white truffle) and the other is right here in Perigord. That makes Monsieur Martin a special sort of geezer!

Our famous friend hunts for truffles, but regrettably with dogs. I had a real urge to see pigs searching out this famous fungus, but according to the Monsieur, pigs are almost impossible to control. Their disobedience and overwhelming desire to find the truffles once they have got the scent often causes the loss of the truffle because they scoff them quicker than the farmer can take them away. And let's face it, you don't argue with a big French Porker!

If Monsieur Martin hunts with dogs, then it's OK with us. He has a truffle auction at the end of January when even the great Restaurateurs from Paris turn up to bid for his special delicacy.

He invites us to this auction and promises to show us around his walnut groves. I ask him for his address and; as we shake hands, I tell him that we shall look forward to seeing him at his auction. I hope he doesn't think I am I'm a covert British truffle broker.

Next to us a vegetable seller is trying to get to grips with why Chris is taking intrusive pictures of his sweet white onions. He laughs and makes fun of Chris and I wish that he could pass on some of his good humour to that fiery old Chicken Trader.

The girls seem to be taking advantage of the fresh produce available at this stall and provocatively gesticulate with the freshly dug courgettes (see photo). Chris and I look at each other, certain that our wives are angling for the modelling job on the book's front cover.

Just for a change we are getting hungry and we happen upon a charming little 'salon du thé' which sadly will provide us with our first bad experience – a really dreadful lunch.

The waitress who approaches us after what seem like age, really can't be bothered to talk to us, smile or indeed exist. However, at least she is consistent, as her foul and unpleasant manner is afforded to all other diners, French or English.

Rachel has ordered a cheese and ham baguette, but is told that they have run out of bread, but for some strange reason they can offer toasted bread with ham. Of course, this is lunchtime in France after all! My Cheffy instincts are telling me that the bread must be stale and that the kitchen economist has therefore decided to toast it in an attempt to make a few extra euros.

Rachel bravely accepts the offer from the boorish lady and the rest of us opt for something a little more classy 'Le Croque Monsieur'. Chris, having no shame, asks for some tomato ketchup.

At last it arrives. Rachel's ham on toast resembles a sort of repugnant pizza thing with some muck on top. It is arid and inedible and even the muck on top tastes like muck.

The Croque Monsieurs is also pants. Squares of those packet type things that go in the microwave and then under the grill to finish. These are still cold in the middle and to add insult to injury the beastly lady has forgotten Reevsie's ketchup, despite his affable reminder.

The food remains uneaten and Rachel, who is fluent in French, complains to the lady in a polite and courteous manner.

Her grumbles are met with nonchalant rebuffs and as we leave at least we know that our meal at 'The Shed' will be incontrovertibly superior.

10, 9, 8, 7, 6, 5, 4, 3, 2, 1 Snap (repeat x 14)

En route, we return to the stately palace that is Chateau Monbazillac to show the girls and to buy a few bottles of the great wine to whet the whistle before dinner. Before leaving Fiona has decided that we should have some photos of us taken jumping from the moated wall. Chris is clearly struggling with the concept of 'self timer' and is getting quite irritated with us for not jumping off the wall all together.

Explaining in great detail how Chris and I should hang our towels in order for them not to become damp or smelly, our jaunt on to Trémolat is as exhilarating as ever. In fact the only disappointment on the journey is the brief interruption in the conversation as we wave and shout our hellos to our old mate Robert who is resting on his favourite stick and wearing his favourite clothes. Politely he waves back and Fiona and Rachel continue to counsel Reevsie and me with a whole host of important and potentially life saving laundry guidance.

The girls are as impressed with 'The Shed' as we had been, and we have reserved two opulent and splendid suites for our night of indulgence. Fiona and I have two single beds pushed together. The room is of colonial elegance, with inconceivably thick drapes enveloping aged windows falling out onto views of sculptured gardens.

The colours of our chamber are a mixture of deep reds and greens and the beds are as soft and bouncy as any that I have bounced on. The adjoining boudoir is a regal affair of upright sofas and posh occasional tables. On those posh occasional tables are some posh little chocolates which are quickly and effortlessly consumed.

Chris had earlier bagged the large double bed saying "You've already got kids."
I have no idea what he means!

NB: Chris and Rachel now have a little boy 'George' who is one year old.

"Can we fit this one in somewhere?"
"Of course. I'll place it with the Shed and wives bit,
it's all posh stuff and will blend in seamlessly!!!"

We decide to have a little kippet and arrange to meet for a pre drink drink, pre dinner in Reevsie's Palace later on. Chris and Rachel have an interesting American couple staying in the suite next to them. She is a skinny blonde model type around 25 and He is a very old man. In fact he could be her Great Grandad. Clearly they love each other dearly. He must have a great personality.

A good sleep and a couple of bottles of our sweet white aperitif have loosened us all up nicely and as we peruse the hotel's fine restaurant menu we are treated to fabulous little canapés and Champagne cocktails.

Admittedly Fiona does look a little panicked by the menu and Reevsie reckons her pallet is more gutter than gastronomic. But Reevsie says that – I don't.

On the table next to us in this graceful restaurant are "Cindy doll, and Great Grandad". Tonight she's dressed from head to skirt in Armani, an over the top scarf and palette loads of make up. Still I reckon she's looking at me.

I notice that her pre dinner tasters have arrived and that the poor girl seems hugely out of her depth. She nervously seems to be waiting for the old boy to start eating, not knowing which cutlery to use. Yep it's definitely his personality she's after.

I cruelly nudge Rachel and tell her about her mis-matched neighbours. As Rachel looks across she is caught eye to eye by the American and for the rest of the night Cindy gives Rachel an evil stare.

The food is completely exquisite. We all had cep tarts (to be featured in the book) and Fiona, Reevsie and I had fillet of beef with the gravy served inside the marrowbone.

Fiona commented on the tasty gravy but it was not until after she had eaten it all that we explained that the marrow had been squeezed out of the bone to give the jus such a thick and rich taste.

Desserts included a stellar Rhubarb tart (also to feature in the book), Heavenly chocolate mousses and strawberry and basil sorbet. Strawberry and basil is a truly great combination and one that we struggle to come to terms with at home.

With coffee we are served with miniature petit fours strangely placed on a lump of tree, but never the less exciting and imaginative. They include toffee apples and Champagne sorbet balls.

For some reason known only to God, I decide to ruffle my hair in a bouffant stupor and Reevsie has obligingly taken a photo.

The Restaurant cleared at 9 o'clock. Its now midnight. I hate customers like us and we decide to adjourn to the smoking room to play billiards. The French form of billiards is interesting and tricky to understand. The balls are the same colour and there are no pockets. I don't get it so we are off to bed.

Reevsie later told me that after dinner he had taken a shower and on entering his room he was surprised to see and hear Rachel loudly faking an orgasm on their bed. It seems that after the American girl staying next door had shown her such disdain during dinner Rachel had decided to retaliate and make some noise to irritate her.

Apparently Rachel is quite well practised in the art of faking orgasms.

Monday morning

I wake up feeling a bit groggy - no surprise there then!! It only takes one or two glasses before I start feeling pissed and last night I had four or five!!

My thoughts turn to the weather, more of a curse than a thought really, I tentatively open the shutter to catch a glimpse of…well nothing. The spire I had taken a picture of the evening before isn't visible anymore - its like it's been taken away. BOLLOCKS! FOG!

However much you prepare yourself for bad weather as a photographer; when it arrives you still can't believe it! Don't they know this is a once in a lifetime book project? Help me out here guys!!

We want to capture something of the splendour of this country hotel so you, the reader, can see what level of discomfort and depravation we, the authors, have to go through to bring you this book. And quite frankly fog isn't going to help us.

I quickly get changed and grab my camera bag. The sun looks like it's trying to break through, or maybe that's a bit of whiter fog? I stare at the sky willing it to part and the fog to lift but as usual nothing happens. One day that's going to work for me! I wait patiently for half an hour, the fog lifts a little, just enough to make it look ethereal. Even the birds start singing, the stream is bubbling over millstones - what a fantastic moment! At last I think I'm getting something. It's still too foggy for an overall shot, so I keep in tight and pick out details: one, two, three good shots in a row. The stillness is only shattered by a voice shouting from behind me "Oi! Reevsie, fuck off!!!" I turn around to see the real Naked Chef leaning out of a 16th century château. Mark, looking rougher than an Irish wolfhound on a wet Sunday, has found a tiny window from his bathroom from which to shout ritual abuse. I quickly take his photo before he can squeeze that stomach back through the tiny aperture and deny to the wives that he would ever do such a thing! Busted matey!

I decide to go and see if my wife is up and about - it must be 8.30 by now. As I get to our apartment the air hostess from next door appears, looking immaculate in some designer gear I couldn't even pronounce, let alone distinguish. She shoots me an icy glare, probably jealous of my wife's shattering orgasm from the night before. Not knowing it was a BAFTA award winning moment.

I tilt my longest lens into the erect position and point it towards her, leering suggestively. Absolutely no response.

Mark and I meet in the a gardens. It's still foggy, but bright; good enough for the shots I have planned. We have an appointment with Vincent - the Top Man, the Head Chef, the Man Who Must Be Obeyed, you get the picture. I make a mental note not to piss him off with sarcastic English humour. Unfortunately Mark doesn't make the same promise as he (The Rosbif) proceeds to give him a lifetime's advice "You don't want to do it like that, you want to do it like this". "Luckily Vincent is a top bloke who knows Mark is only winding him up - one Master Chef to another! And he takes it all in his stride.

4 TARTS

It was our idea is to let a French chef, namely Vincent, pick three of his favourite tarts, as we know whatever he cooks is going to be superb. We weren't disappointed. The fourth tart will be our choice!! I think you'll agree she's a cracker!!! Vincent has made a mushroom or rather Cép tart, along with a very nice nice tomato version, followed by a sweet rhubarb tart with a mango sorbet accompaniment.

We have made a lovely young lady dress up in beret, basque, fishnets.....

Disclaimer: 'She really is from Essex!'

We turn the garden into a make-shift studio. For the photographers amongst you I'm using a single Bowens 250 esprit head with a small softbox, a Bowens zip disk reflector to enhance the daylight, coupled with a four year old Kodak D760 digital camera and Nikon 105mm f2 and 85mm shift and tilt lenses. The camera is a bit of a technological dinosaur but is one of my favourites. There's something very industrial about it and anyway it still does the job.

Our first task is to photograph Vincent. He's a bit reluctant, but after arm twisting he gives in. Meanwhile the girls go off to get us some breakfast. They arrange for croissants and sweet cakes, tea and coffee which we all tuck into outside. The girls take pictures of us, taking pictures of Vincent. Just before the tarts arrive we decide it's not a bad idea to show Freddy and Co some of the pictures we have already taken as they have no idea who or what we are. They are being very hospitable and one has to say very trusting. The reaction is good. I think it gave us a bit of credibility. Mark talks through his choice of ingredients and inspirations for the recipes he has chosen to include.

Poire Williams Pear poached in an aged armagnac and red wine aperitif from the market
Serves: 2

Here is what you need:

2x Poire Williams Pears
500ml Aged armagnac and red wine aperitif
500ml Red wine
50g Caster sugar

What you need to do to it:

1. Pour the armagnac aperitif, red wine and sugar into a pot and boil.
2. Turn down heat to a simmer and add pears.
3. Cover with a piece of parchment paper.
4. Simmer for approximately 30 minutes or until the pears are slightly soft.
5. Leave to cool in their own liquid.
6. What to do with the extra liquid?
   a) Poach more pears.
   b) Pour it over ice cream.
   c) Drink it!

NB: *Our neighbours at the farm next door laughed at this recipe - and said "Just pour neat eau de vie over prunes!"*

Prunes in Eau de Vie
Serves: 2

Here is what you need:

Prunes
Sugar
Water
Eau de Vie
Crème fraiche

What you need to do to it:

1. If you can get hold of some half cooked prunes then you simply put both prunes and eau de vie in a jar and that's it. Although DON'T fill to the top as the prunes will expand and will try & escape out of the jar.

2. If you can't get hold of half cooked prunes then dried ones will do but take 100g of sugar, add it to 100ml of boiling water and stir until all sugar is dissolved. Then take the prunes and equal quantities of the syrup solution and eau de vie and pour over the prunes in the jar.

3. Serve with crème fraiche.

Not wishing to sound too clichéd but everything is great - the grounds look fantastic, my wife is laughing and joking with Fiona. Mark is eating the tarts and enjoying himself more than ever and I'm photographing for fun. What a fantastic morning, one of the highlights of doing this book! The sun comes out and adds a sparkle to the last few shots. By twelve it's all done. A quick pack and load up the van and we are ready to go. We wish we could stay longer, but we haven't exactly given ourselves a lot of time before we need to start making our way home. Before we drop the girls back at the airport the all important shop for tinned peas has to be done. Now I know we are in France cooking gastronomic delights, but there's something about French tinned veg that the wife and I love. Mark and Fi probably think we are stupid and they're probably right, but they still buy some themselves. We cap off the day with a Gallic McDonald's.

Mint Choc Chip Ice Cream
Serves:2

Here is what you need

450ml	Full fat milk
450ml	Double cream
150g	Caster Sugar
100ml	Créme de Menthe
50g	Dark chocolate
10x	Large egg yolks (Free range!)

The great thing about Bergerac is that everything is nearby, the airport is only 15 minutes away and as we roll up to the front door it is sunny and clear and the girls should have an easy journey home if the weather is like this all the way.

They refuse to wear their hats so to embarrass them one more time we wear ours! After a quick kiss and a cuddle we depart the airport heading back to the gite. It's depressing to know that by the time we leave this evening for our mammoth drive home the girls will already be back in England.

Our task was simply to follow the instructions for leaving the gite. Not as easy as it sounds if you see Tony's list, added to this Rachel's and Fiona's instructions on how to hang the towels out on the washing line. They're so convinced we're going to get it wrong we have to take a photo on the phone and send it to them!

What you need to do to it:

1. Boil milk and cream in a thick bottom saucepan.
2. Seperate egg yolks and whisk with caster sugar.
3. When milk and cream have boiled pour a quater of the mixture onto the sugar and eggs – then stir with a wooden spoon.
4. Pour the liquid back into pan, mix together and cook slowly until it thickens. Stir continually and don't allow it to boil or eggs will split.
5. Stir the warm "Créme Anglaise" until the consistency is thick enough to cover the back of your wooden spoon.
6. Strain the Créme Anglaise into a bowl over another bowl filled with ice.
7. Stir and cool the Créme Anglaise.
8. Chop up the chocolate.
9. Pour the Créme Anglaise into the ice cream turner and just before the ice cream sets throw in the chopped chocolate.
10. Continue to churn, remove and enjoy!

It's nearly quarter to six and we are done. The house is packed up for the winter. In fact we are probably going to be the next people here in January, but that's another story.

The weather is still clear, the sun is on its way down and we are on our way home. The aim for tonight is to get as near to Paris as possible before having a kip somewhere.

As we drive through some really picturesque villages on our way to the motorway we reflect on what we have achieved, probably more than either of us imagined. It's been a fantastic trip. Even though we are both back at work the day after tomorrow; far from feeling unenthusiastic, it really has motivated us both.

It's now 8 o'clock and Mark's turn to drive. It's Haircut 100 for the next hour and a half and we agree that we will keep each other awake the rest of the way. By 9.30pm we are both hungry. The service station at Châteaux Rue is still serving food so after filling up with fuel we partake of our favourite dish, ham chips and béarnaise sauce. Spirits are still high, so for a laugh we wear our dayglo orange hats and laugh like naughty school boys. After sending Fi a picture on the phone we get a reply from Mark's Mum (who was looking after the kids). It simply said "Idiots!" Thanks Mum but not unwarranted!

After a couple of strong coffees and a debate on "Is that waitress just good looking or would we class her as filthy?" (a conversation only faithful married men are allowed to have), we climb aboard the Tonka truck and head ever nearer to Paris. I'm driving, so it's now Nik Kershaw on the 80s revival night.

Motorway driving in the dark is boring and most of all tiring. It's so easy to fix your vision on the rear lights of the guy in front and follow them. This obviously leads to confusion when he's not going the same way as you!

It's now midnight. If only it went as quickly as reading it out loud. We are both knackered, tired, a little dazed and confused. We are just short of Paris and decide to drive through, but before we do, it's fuel time once again. At this multiplex service station, in God only knows where, we find a unexpected treat . . . two vibrating massage chairs and only two euros a go. Mark has a glint in his eye as the school boy re-emerges and he's off. I go and get two coffees. On my return I am greeted with what can only be described as chef porn, cries of delight, reminiscent of Meg Ryan in When Harry Met Sally, amble across the garage shop not wanting to miss out, jump into the other chair and stick the money in the slot. Imagine the scene, two Englishmen at midnight getting a massage in Paris, in cries of ecstasy (or was that agony). It must have been good as I spilt my coffee!

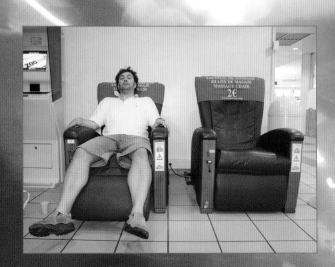

I don't know what was more embarrassing having that much fun with a mate or being pummelled by a mechanical chair and enjoying it. Anyway the fun is over and the more serious side of driving has reared its ugly head, it's nearly twelve thirty and now Mark's turn to drive.

Mark...
Killed a fly.
We drive through Gay Paris. It's pretty quiet at this time of the day in the metropolis and I have now decided that I hate Nik Kershaw.

Leaving the bewitching and beautiful gentle countryside behind we seem to be making good time. Reevsie, as ever is in a Photo Frenzy. This time he is shooting blurred images of passing night trucks, bridges and motorway lights.

He doesn't. He throws them back and I am reassured that Captain Big Bladder is human after all.

We have an ongoing agreement between ourselves not to sleep while the other is driving and the kilometres are gobbled up as the 'inside truck banter' turns from boring to completely ragged.

"Name three Spandau Ballet hits from '84".

Chris tries in vain to educate his stupid friend on key aspects of history including Agincourt, Charles de Gaulle and various victories over the French. I hadn't realized he was so intelligent, but he's probably making it up anyway.

The journey home is passing quickly now. Both of us are tired but jubilant and with good natured quarrels over '10 Abba hits and Elton John songs' we suddenly become aware that we have completely missed the Calais turn off. Never mind, Lens is a great town at 3 o'clock in the morning!

At long last we arrive at Calais. Its 4.06 am. And there's a Ferry at 4.30. What luck! We are pulled over and searched and Reevsie is worried that the Customs man is going to confiscate his jars of peas. His worries are unfounded. We are waved through and board the boat for our journey home.

It's a quiet old ferry this one – No sign of day trippers here. The moaning canteen worker tells us that the total tally for this crossing is eight cars, two coaches and one truck. Still the café is open and we help ourselves to a Full English.

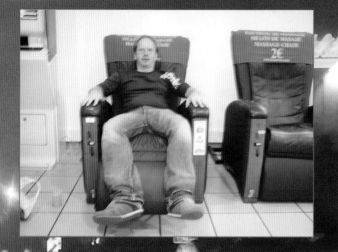

Somewhere North we have pulled into a truck stop. I wonder what cargo the monstrous sleeping lorries might be carrying as I dive into a hedge to relieve myself. My ponderings turn to amazement that Captain Big Bladder has still not found it necessary to go for a wee. Actually this type of bladder control is causing me to consider the possibility that Reevsie is not human – an alien maybe. I remind myself to keep an eye out for any other unworldly characteristics.

We continue to stroll about stretching those aching muscles and after picking some crab apples from a nearby tree I decide to launch them at Reevsie. Perhaps it is my need to see if he will exterminate these incoming ballistic fruits with the radio active and devilish eyes of an invader from space.

The crossing passes uneventfully and after copious amounts of coffee the White Cliffs scream out a welcome to us. It is 5.30am. We roll off the ferry and don't get stopped by customs. Slightly disappointing as I was looking forward to Reevsie explaining his pea fetish.

It's raining, grey, dingy, dark and depressing. The A20 is chokka and the M25 is snarled up. Those fearful yellow road lights on our cramped roads are playing havoc with Reevsie's contact lenses and the intermittent windscreen wipers are beginning to annoy me.

I suddenly realise that I am in a bad mood and Reevsie is getting seriously annoyed with that woman on Radio 2.

I drop Chris off in Colchester at 7.30am. We have been up for nearly 24 hours and Rachel has already left for her day's work in London.

I call Fiona who asks "Are you in Paris yet?"

At least I get to see my girls before they go off to school. Then I hit my bed for a couple of hours, dreaming of a place called Perigord.

My dreams are shattered by the realization that it's back to work tomorrow!

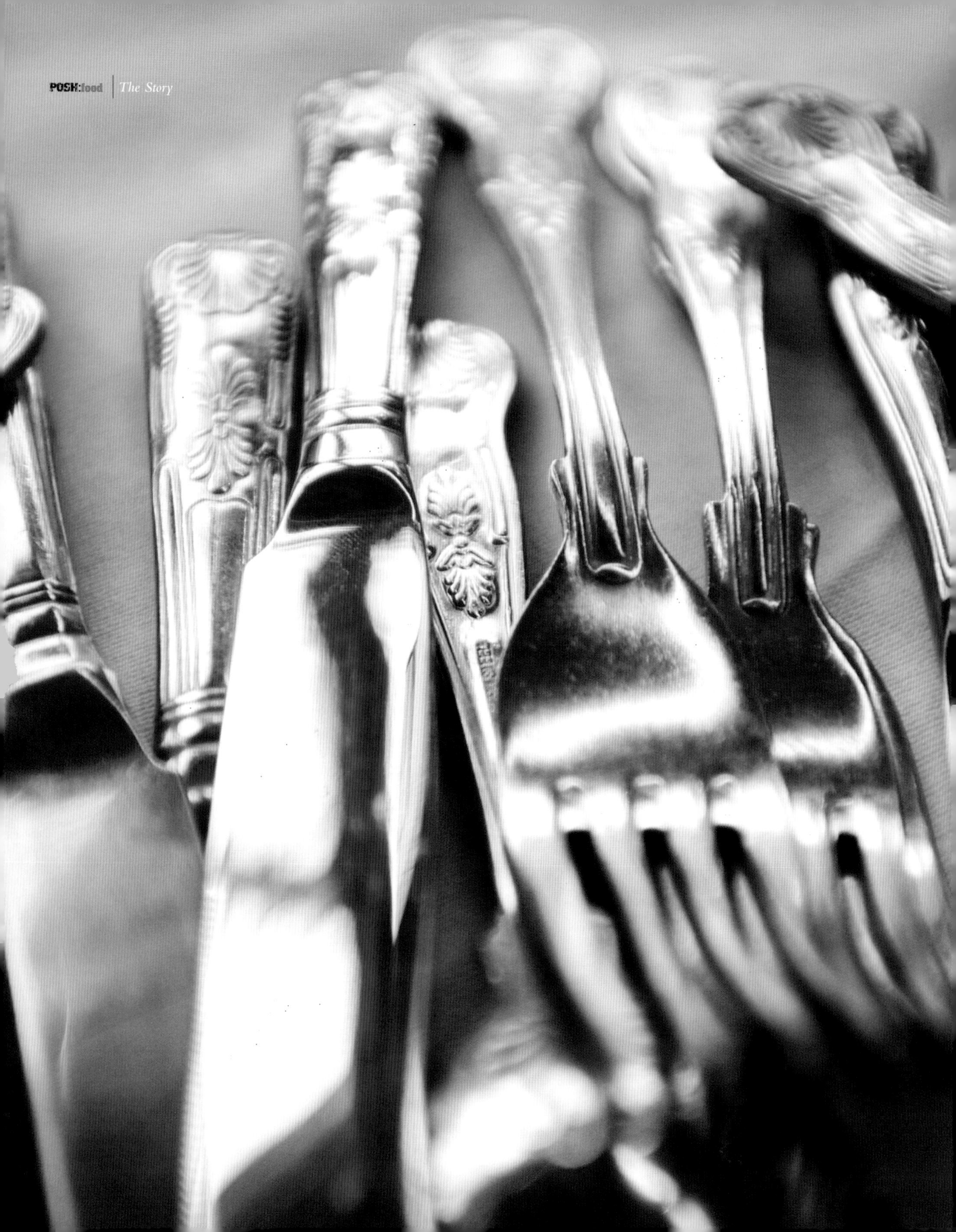

Inter

The Cheesy bit, not quite the dessert. The restaurant.

course

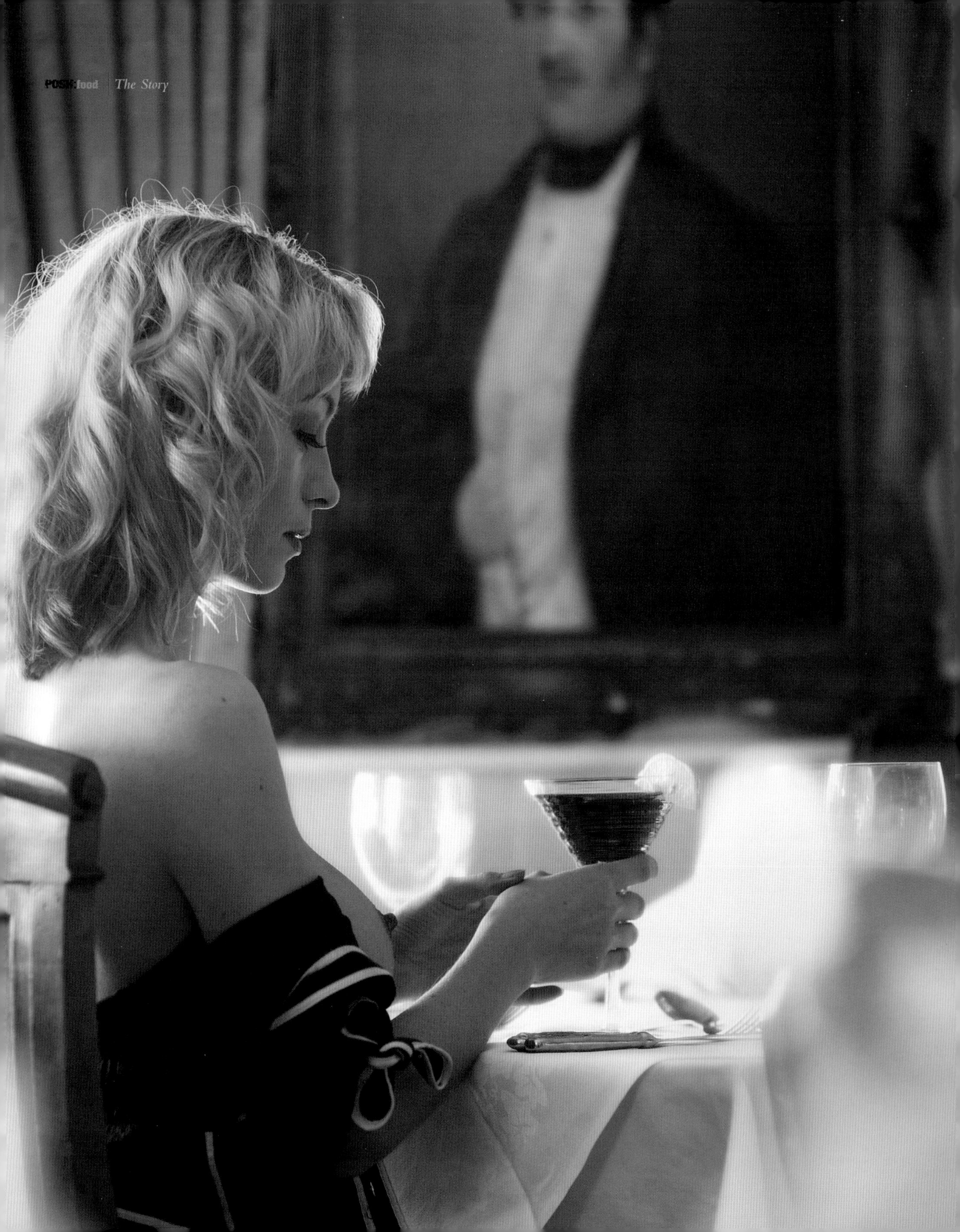

The Restaurant

It's now a month since we've been back home and the Dordogne is but a distant memory. Life at the restaurant is as hectic as usual, seventy for lunch and as many as eighty for service tonight.

It's taken Reevsie over a month to edit the photos and he's still at it. We have also found ourselves a new member of the team, a designer by the name of Neil. A client and friend of the ginger one, who had been advising us on the project. It suddenly hit us that we've found our man. How could he refuse our offer to design the book in every spare moment he has for the next year and a half for no pay! "But we will give you a share of the profits!" we said. 'That's a third of nothing!'

The deal was duly done, so it was back to the arduous task of cooking and photographing.

There were so many recipes that I wanted to do in France, but there just wasn't time to do everything we wanted while we were out there, so over some of the following pages please enjoy those that we missed.

One of the first things we wanted to prepare was the English breakfast and we did this on the same morning that Reevsie's brother Andy painted gold leaf onto our cornflakes (see recipe). No trick photography there I assure you !

Obviously it took four attempts to cook the breakfast. One for each of us and one for the photo!

The rest of the 'Stupid Millionaire range' followed thus. I even tried to teach Reevsie how to pluck a pheasant - and yes I did say 'pluck!' It didn't go quite to plan. Grave robbers have more finesse!

The other recipes are simply our favourites or like the rest of the book, pure self indulgence. So guys, get off your backside and impress the women with your newfound culinary skills. Good luck!

So you have decided to become a butcher

1 Cut through and remove winglets.

2 Using the point of a sharp knife release the breasts from the body.

3 'Tease' the breast outward from the bone.

4 Your breasts should look like this – note I have "cleaned" the bone of the pheasant.

5 Breast added to the hot pot (with butter and oil) – presentation side down first.

6 Breast turned over – note ball bearing (shot) in photo 6 – watch teeth.

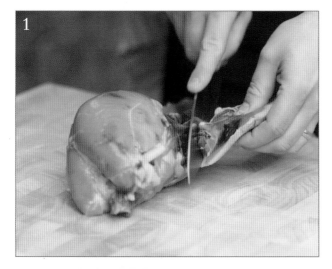

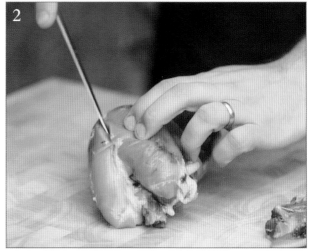

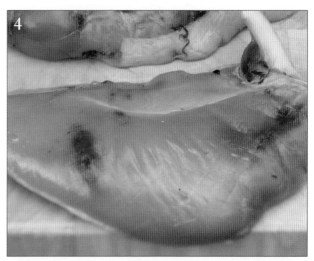

A great alternative to chicken, pheasant is a super tasting bird and is served as simply as possible – in this case with sweet, pickled red cabbage.

I tried to teach Chris how to pluck and prepare a pheasant for this recipe but he made a total cock-up of it (see previous pages!) It is probably best to buy two oven ready pheasant breasts.

Pan Roasted Pheasant with Pickled Red Cabbage
Serves:2

Here is what you need:

	A little cooking oil
	A knob of butter
2x	Nice plump pheasant breasts (skins removed)
2x	Slices smoked back bacon
	Salt and Pepper

What you need to do to it:

1. Heat a frying pan with a little cooking oil and a knob of butter.
2. Season pheasant breasts with salt and pepper (both sides)
3. Place the breasts in the pan and allow to colour for 2 minutes.
4. Turn over and colour other side for a further 1 minute.
5. Place a slice of bacon on each breast (pheasants) and place in a hot oven (220°C fan assisted/Gas mark 7) for approx 10 minutes. The tip here is that when the bacon is coloured, the breasts will be cooked.
6. Take out of the oven, allow to rest for 5 minutes then slice and serve on the warmed red cabbage.

Pickled Red Cabbage

Here is what you need:

500g	Red cabbage – thinly sliced
50ml	White wine vinegar
100g	Sultanas
100g	Brown sugar
1x	Large red onion – thinly sliced
1x	Bay leaf
	Salt and Pepper

Make the pickled red cabbage a day or so in advance.

What you need to do to it:

1. In a pot heat a little cooking oil (enough to just cover the base of the pot).
2. Add the sliced onions and cabbage and stir well.
3. Add the brown sugar, salt and pepper and white wine vinegar.
4. Cook on a slow heat until the cabbage is as soft as you like it (up to 30 mins), but add a splash of water if the cabbage and vinegar juices are reducing too quickly.
5. Stir often.
6. When soft, toss in the sultanas, adjust seasoning and store till needed.

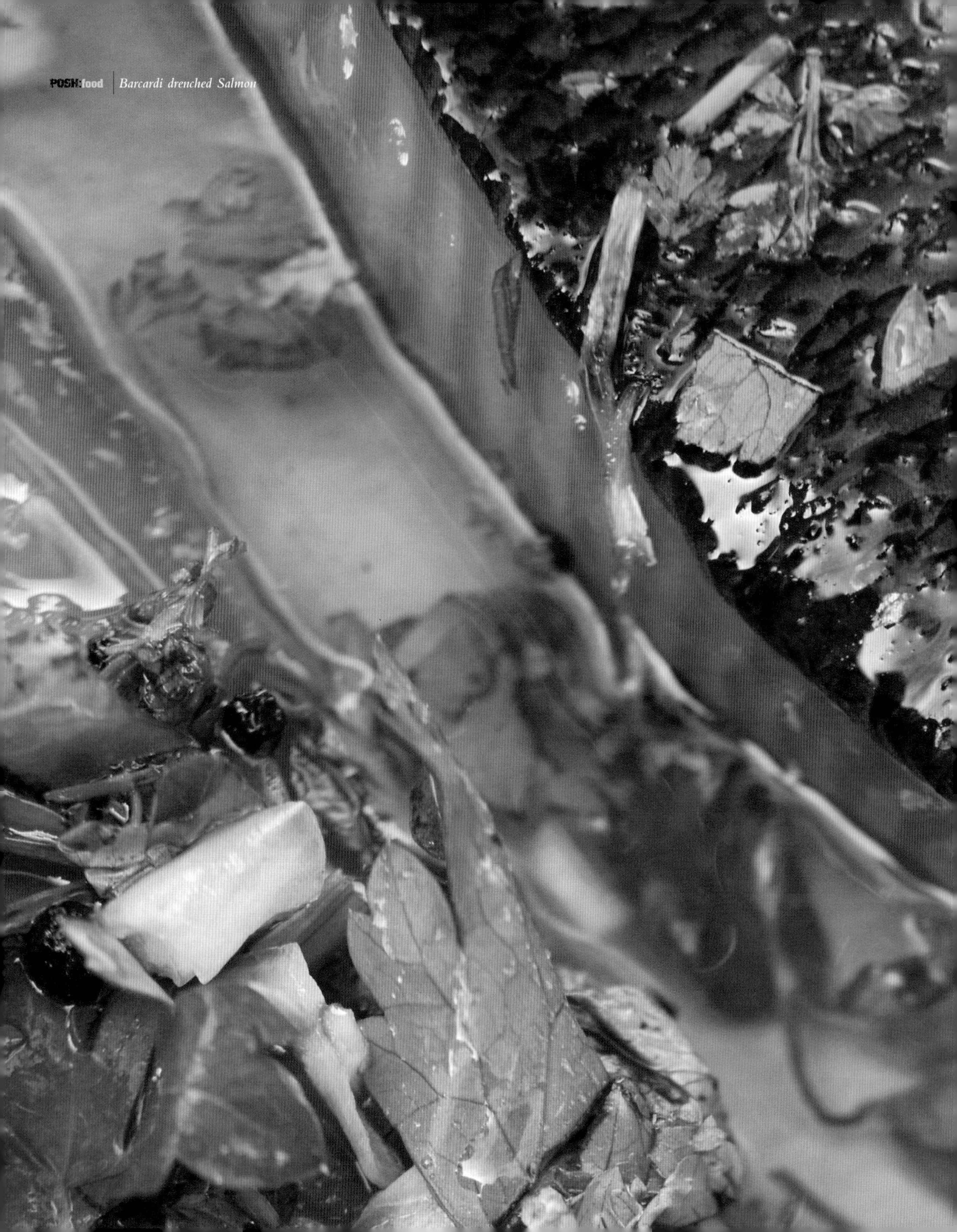

Salmon & Bacardi

I really have no idea how this concoction came into my head. I don't even like Bacardi that much. But it really really works and is totally gorgeous.

It takes a week and 5 minutes to make. 5 minutes to make the marinade, and a week to leave it to 'cook' in the marinade.

Bacardi drenched Salmon
Serves:6

Here is what you need:

600g REALLY fresh salmon – ask your friendly fishmonger to 'pin bone' it and 'scale' it but leave the skin on. If he's a misery, call me and I will do it for you (Joking).

200g Caster sugar

50g Sea salt flakes

200ml Bacardi

1x Mans handful fresh coriander

1x Teaspoon cracked black pepper

1x Banana shallot – roughly chopped

What you need to do to it:

1. Gently score the skin of the salmon in 5 places (to allow the marinade to penetrate).

2. Place the salmon in a lipped tray.

3. Make the marinade by mixing the sugar, salt, coriander, shallots, Bacardi and black pepper in a bowl.

4. Spread the marinade over the top of the salmon skin and push down evenly.

5. Cover with tin foil and weigh down (with something like a heavy Pyrex dish).

6. Place in the fridge.

7. Turn the salmon over twice a day and baste with the marinade. You will notice that the thickish marinade will become liquid as the salt and sugar react together.

8. After 7 days, pour off the marinade. Pat dry and chop some more coriander.

9. Spread the coriander over the salmon – it is now ready.

10. It can be carved very thinly and served with a little lime or served with mashed pea crème fraiche.

I really adore these onions. In the summer we eat loads of them at home with burgers on the BBQ or with hot dogs etc.

Here I have used them with bangers and bubble and squeak mash (see below) but make more than you need as they keep really well and reheat perfectly. Be careful though, as they do make you fart a bit!

Caramelized White Onions (and chilli)
Serves: 6

Here is what you need:

4x Large onions (approx 1kg)
100ml Olive oil
200g Brown sugar
30ml White wine vinegar
 Salt and pepper
 Chilli flakes (optional)

What you need to do to it:

1. Slice the onions as thinly as possible.
2. Heat the olive oil in a pan.
3. Add the onions and 'sweat' down until soft and slightly coloured.
4. Add the white wine vinegar and the brown sugar.
5. Continue to cook till almost all the juice is dissolved.
6. Season with salt and pepper and chilli flakes if you are brave enough.

Traditionally bubble and squeak is made out of leftovers – including beef bits - and then fried. I think the texture of bubble and squeak mash with pork and leek sausages and a dollop of English mustard is a marriage made in heaven. And for an added thrill, pile on some of my caramelized onions.

Bubble and Squeak Mash (to go with Pork Sausages)
Serves:6

Here is what you need:

1x Knob of butter
2-3 Large potatoes (approx 600g)
150g Savoy cabbage
1x Red onion (I like the colour)
 Half a clove of garlic – crushed
3x Slices of back bacon – cubed
 Worcester sauce – a splash to taste
2x Teaspoon English mustard
100 – 200ml Double cream

What you need to do to it:

1. Peel and boil the potatoes then mash and store.
2. Shred the cabbage into little pieces, boil in salted water and drain.
3. Shred the onion and crush the garlic.
4. Chop the bacon into little pieces.
5. Melt the butter in a frying pan and cook the bacon till nicely coloured.
6. Add the onions and garlic and stir.
7. Add the blanched cabbage.
8. Season with salt, pepper, Worcester sauce and English mustard.
9. Add to the mashed potato.
10. Add the double cream and beat all together.

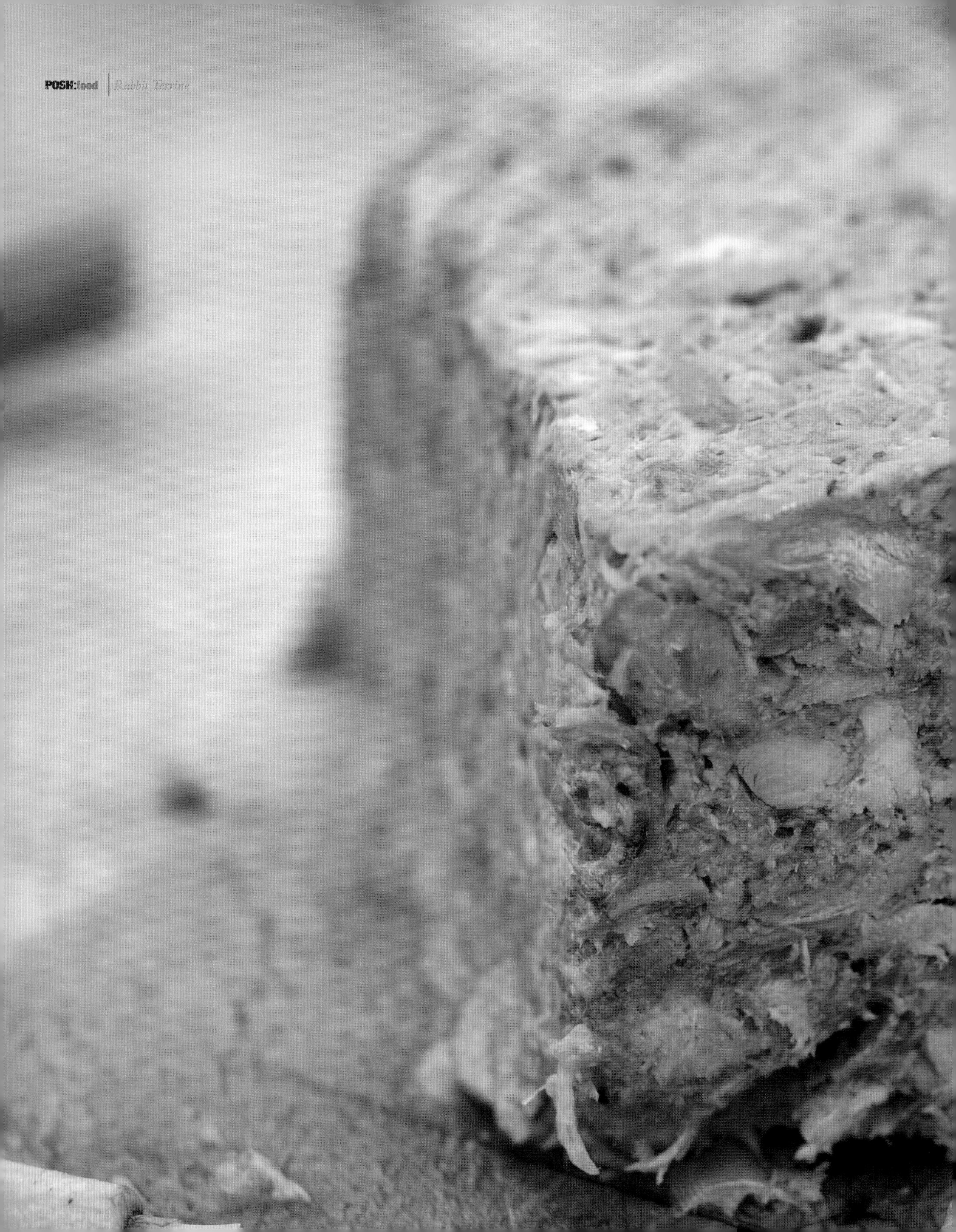

Rabbit Terrine

Yes I know, this looks horribly complicated and long winded and ….

Well, you're right, but we do want to impress our guests!

You will need a fairly large and deep braising tray (the one you use for the Christmas turkey) – mine measures about 40cm long by 26cm wide by 9cm deep. And a terrine mould – mine measures about 25cm long by 10cm wide by 8cm deep (and so does the mould).

Pressed Rabbit
and Bacon Terrine
Serves:8

Here is what you need:

2x	Whole rabbits – skinned and oven ready
1.5kg	Belly of pork – diced
1x	Head garlic – peeled
4x	Bay leaves
1x	Large onion – roughly chopped
	Cooking oil or duck fat
2x	Sprigs fresh thyme
2x	Sprigs fresh rosemary
	Salt and cracked black pepper

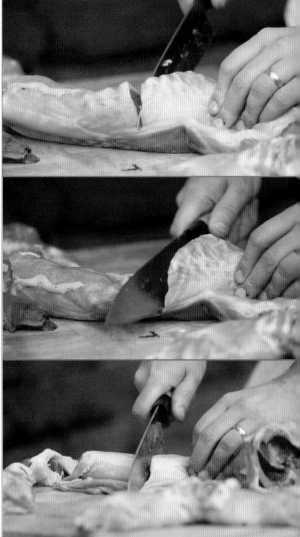

What you need to do to it:

1. Chop everything up, season with salt and pepper and place in a braising dish.

2. Pour over enough oil to cover the ingredients (this will seem like loads of oil, but you can strain it and use it again after).

3. Cover with tin foil and place in a warm oven temperature (170°C fan assisted/Gas mark 3) to braise gently for about 3 hours.

4. With a fork, check the progress of braising. When the meat falls off the bones the dish can come out of the oven.

5. Allow the meat to cool in the cooking oil then strain and flake the meat into a clean bowl.

6. Line the terrine mould with cling film.

7. Slightly mash the meats together with the braised onions and garlic, but discard the herbs.

8. Adjust the seasoning and squash the meat into the terrine mould.

9. Weigh down with heavy things (jam jars etc) and refrigerate for at least 24 hours.

10. Turn out the terrine, slice and serve with crusty bread, chutney and salad.

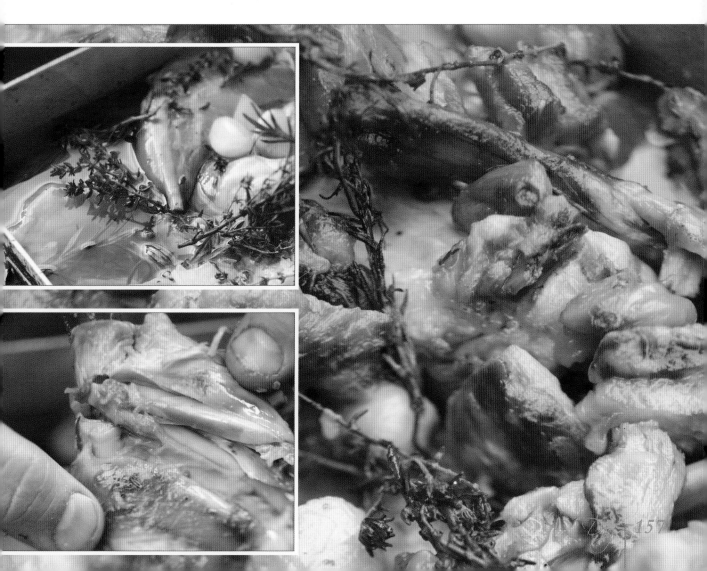

PLAYBOY meets BUNNY

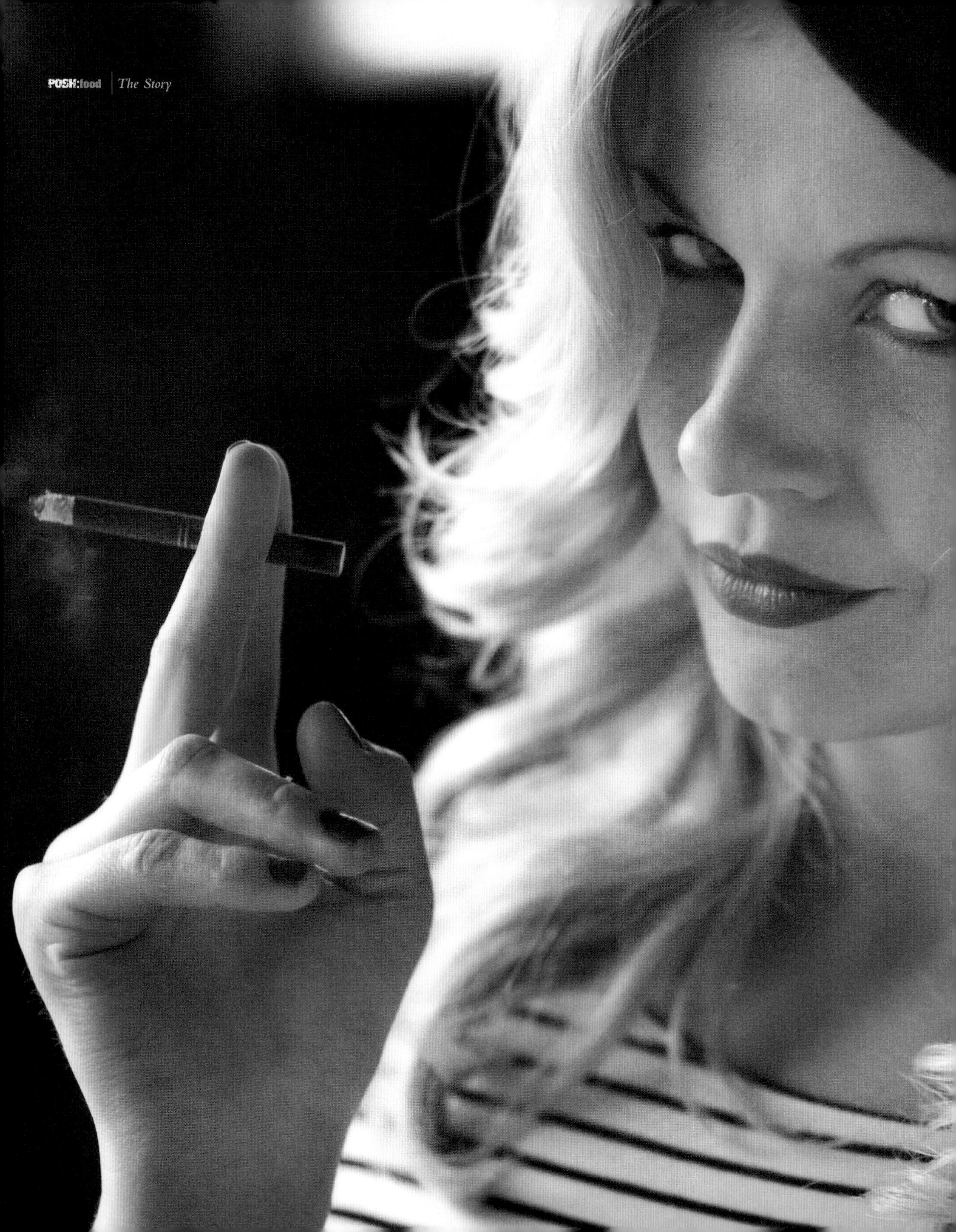

STUPID MILLIONAIRES

Indulgence
&
Filth

this doesn't mean you!

The Stupid Millionaires

On arriving home the idiotic notion of 'The Stupid Millionaires range' of foods has once again reared its head.

What had started out as an amusing diversion has gathered pace and manifested itself into some fairly zany recipes.

These particular offerings are strictly designed for the very wealthy as they include ingredients that we (the common man) could never afford and back at the Brasserie we have had loads of fun developing these ideas.

We deemed it necessary to purchase the very best caviar to accompany the vodka ice lollies and to employ the very pretty young models that make that particular dish look so appetising!

The golden cornflakes are hideously expensive as we needed to enlist the help of Reevsie's brother – a London silversmith - to hand paint each flake with real gold leaf!

The banana custard is finished with a sabayon made from the finest bubbly and as for the Stupid Millionaires pizza ….. well it is piled high with foie gras and almost vulgar amounts of Perigord truffles!

Enjoy this indulgence. If you are adventurous enough then follow the recipes or if you are rich enough then get in touch!

STUPID MILLIONAIRE$
Gold cornflakes
Serves:2

Here is what you need:

Kellogg's Cornflakes
Gold Leaf
Golden Syrup (Tate & Lyle)
1x Goldsmith
Jersey Double Cream

What you need to do to it:

1. Take a handful of cornflakes making sure that none is broken.
2. Mix a dessertspoon of syrup and 2 dessertspoons of boiling water (in a bowl) to make an edible adhesive.
3. Get 1 Goldsmith to paint each flake with a flat sided brush (one side only) with sugar syrup.
4. Apply gold leaf to each glued flake.
5. Take 4 bowls, filled with normal cornflakes, sprinkle over golden flakes & drench under thick Jersey Cream. Eat while reading Financial Times, and pondering which convertible car to buy your mistress.

Now here's the thing – it's the last day at the gite, we are hungry and still have a few bits of veg left – so I made a wonderful chunky vegetarian soup with a twist – chicken stock and foie gras – enjoy!!

STUPID MILLIONAIRE$ Decadent left over Vegetable Soup

Serves:2

Here is what you need:

1x   Red pepper (chilli)
1x   Medium leek
2x   Small carrots
1x   Jerusalem artichoke
2x   Shallots
4x   Green beans
1x   Small handful of peas
1x   Flat mushroom
1x   Small potato
    Chives
    Splash of olive oil
    Salt and pepper

What you need to do to it:

1. Peel the veg and potatoes and roughly chop everything.
2. In a pan, heat a little olive oil and gently sweat all the vegetables (except peas and chives).
3. Season with salt and pepper.
4. Add enough chicken stock just to cover and simmer (Until all vegetables are soft).
5. Top up stock as needed.
6. Throw in peas and chives, lay over a slab of foie gras and have a photo taken.

STUPID MILLIONAIRE$ Pizza

Serves:4 (15cm-20cm) Pizzas

For the truly decadent among you, we are delighted to present this thin-based offering spilling with truffles, cheese and fois gras. If you can't be bothered to make it, and indeed are a stupid millionaire, please feel free to call and I shall be happy to negotiate a price for your dinner party!

Failing this, here's the recipe.

Here is what you need

Pizza base

500g	Plain flour
1x	Tablespoon sea salt
1x7g	Pack dried yeast
300ml	Warm water
1x	Tablespoon olive oil
1x	Tablespoon chives, diced
1x	Tablespoon oregano, chopped
1x	Tablespoon Maldon Sea Salt

Pizza tomato puree (to go on the base)

4x	Large beef tomatoes, plunged in boiling water, skinned and roughly chopped
100g	Tomato puree
150ml	Expensive red wine
1x	Large white onion, peeled and roughly chopped
1x	Head fresh garlic, peeled and roughly chopped
1x	Tablespoon red wine vinegar
2x	Tablespoon brown sugar
1x	Tablespoon fresh oregano, roughly chopped
1x	Crushed black pepper
1x	Tablespoon Maldon Sea Salt

For the topping

10x	Cep or chestnut mushrooms, sliced
2x	Red onions, sliced
1x	Large avocado, peeled and chopped
1x	Tablespoon fresh chives, chopped
1x	Large red pepper, sliced
1x	Large green pepper, sliced
200g	Saucisson sec (or chorizo), sliced
200g	Emmenthal cheese, finely grated
100g	Foie gras, sliced
2x	Black perigord truffles, finely sliced
1x	Tablespoon Maldon Sea Salt
1x	Pepper
1x	Olive oil

What you need to do to is on the following page

Day 173

STUPID MILLIONAIRE$ Pizza
Continued...

What you need to do to it:

Make the tomato puree paste.

1. Warm a spoonful of olive oil in a thick bottomed pan then add the chopped onions and garlic.
2. Sweat them for a couple of minutes then add the chopped tomatoes.
3. Stir in the garlic, tomato puree, salt, pepper and herbs.
4. Add your best red wine, red wine vinegar and brown sugar.
5. Reduce as slowly as possible (on the lowest heat) until the puree is nice and thick and of good coating consistency.
6. Cool it down then refrigerate until needed

To make the bases.

1. Put a tablespoon of the flour in a bowl with 3 tablespoons of warm water then sprinkle in the yeast and mix until the yeast is dissolved.
2. Let the yeast mix activate for about 10 minutes – it will become a little frothy – then add the sea salt, the remaining flour, the water, the olive oil and the herbs.
3. Mix all really well. I did it by hand but a mixer with a dough hook is really helpful. Once well mixed turn out onto a floured table and knead for a further 10 minutes.
4. Put the dough back in the bowl and brush with a little olive oil to stop it drying out and cover with cling film.
5. Leave it in a warm kitchen for about an hour until it has swollen to twice the size.
6. Once risen, take the dough out and knock it back to release the air and cut into 4 even pieces.
7. Mould the pieces into balls and leave on a floured surface covering with cling film for another half an hour.
8. Then flatten the balls into flying saucers and roll (with a fine bottle of wine) thinly until each base is approx. 20cm wide.

For the topping

(which can be prepared when the pizza dough is proving).

1. Prepare, peel, de-seed and chop all the vegetables and grate the cheese.
2. Heat a little olive oil in a pan and fry the peppers, then the onions and then the mushrooms – just until they are slightly soft (no more than a couple of minutes).
3. Season with salt and pepper and cool, to put on the top of the pizzas when we are ready.
4. Don't prepare the avocado until the last minute or it will discolour.

Building the pizzas.

1. Heat the oven to maximum heat (this one was 220°C fan assisted/Gas mark 7).
2. Put the pizza base on oven proof parchment paper.
3. Spread the puree thinly over the base leaving a couple of centimetres around the edge.
4. Top with some of the prepared onions, mushrooms peppers, saucisson and avocado.
5. Sprinkle with some of the cheese and season with salt and pepper.
6. Pick the pizza and the parchment paper up and place in the hot oven.
7. Cook for 3-4 minutes.
8. Take out and add some of the truffles and foie gras and drizzle a little olive oil over.
9. Cook for a further 4 minutes.
10. Take out, drizzle over a little more olive oil, then sprinkle on some lovely chopped herbs.
11. Prepare the other pizzas the same way.

This silly little idea sprung into my head one night when I was in bed. Strangely enough I seem to have some of my best ideas in bed, the bath or out on my jet ski.

Banana custard used to be a favourite and now, although this recipe seems long winded and complicated, it is actually quite simple to make, up to a couple of days before you want to eat it. What takes a little more skill is the champagne sabayon that I've used as the sauce for the dish. But if you don't want to bother with the sabayon just melt some chocolate and use it for a sauce or mash up some raspberries with some sugar as a melba sauce – or just warm through some lovely Tiptree jam!

STUPID MILLIONAIRES
Banana Custard with champagne
Serves: 4

Here is what you need:

1x Blow torch
4x 'Cheffy' stainless steel egg rings measuring 7.4cm wide by 4cm deep
3x Large bananas
1x Thin flat sponge (enough to cover the base of the 4 rings)
600g (or 4 x 150g pots) of Ambrosia Devon custard
2x Leaves gelatine – don't use powder – it's pants!
2x Vanilla pods
4x Teaspoons of really good strawberry jam (Tiptree Jam)

A glass of your best champagne (drink what's not used!)

What you need to do to it:

1. Use the stainless steel rings to cut out a layer of thin sponge and leave in the base of the ring.
2. Soak the gelatine leaves in a little cold water.
3. Spread some jam on the sponges (in the base of the rings).
4. Splash the sponges with a little champagne.
5. Open up the cartons of custard and slice open the vanilla pod.
6. Scrape out the beans from the vanilla and mix with the custard.
7. Strain the gelatine leaves leaving just enough water to cover them and warm through in a little pan until they turn to liquid. Stir to avoid lumps.
8. Slice the 'nanas and put a layer in each ring (on top of sponges).
9. Mix the now melted gelatine liquid with the custard and whisk well.
10. Spoon the custard over the first layer of bananas.
11. Repeat.
12. Leave in fridge to set, at least 24 hours.

When ready to serve, the banana custard can be placed on a plate and gently persuaded out by warming the sides of the egg ring with a blow torch – not too long though, or it will melt!

Serve with a sauce of your choice or ….. try my sabayon. The sabayon can be made a little before your guests arrive or he/she gets back from work.

Sabayon
Serves:4

Here is what you need:

6x Egg yolks
5x Tablespoons of champagne (if you haven't drunk it!)
5x Tablespoons of caster sugar
Balloon whisk
Bowl to cook it in
Larger bowl half filled with ice (bigger than the bowl you are cooking the sabayon in)

What you need to do to it:

1. Cream the yolks, sugar and champagne together in a bowl over a saucepan of gently simmering water (cheffy term – bain marie or water bath).
2. Whisk for a good 5 to 10 minutes until the mix starts to thicken and grow in volume. Do not stop whisking or the eggs will scramble. Also do not let the mix get too hot (lower the heat as necessary – the mix should stay at about blood temp).
3. When thick and foamy remove from heat.
4. Place the bowl in the larger one containing ice and carry on whisking till the sabayon is cold and thick.

To Serve:

Surround the banana custard with the sabayon and gently scorch with a blow torch to get a lovely, slightly crispy brown skin.

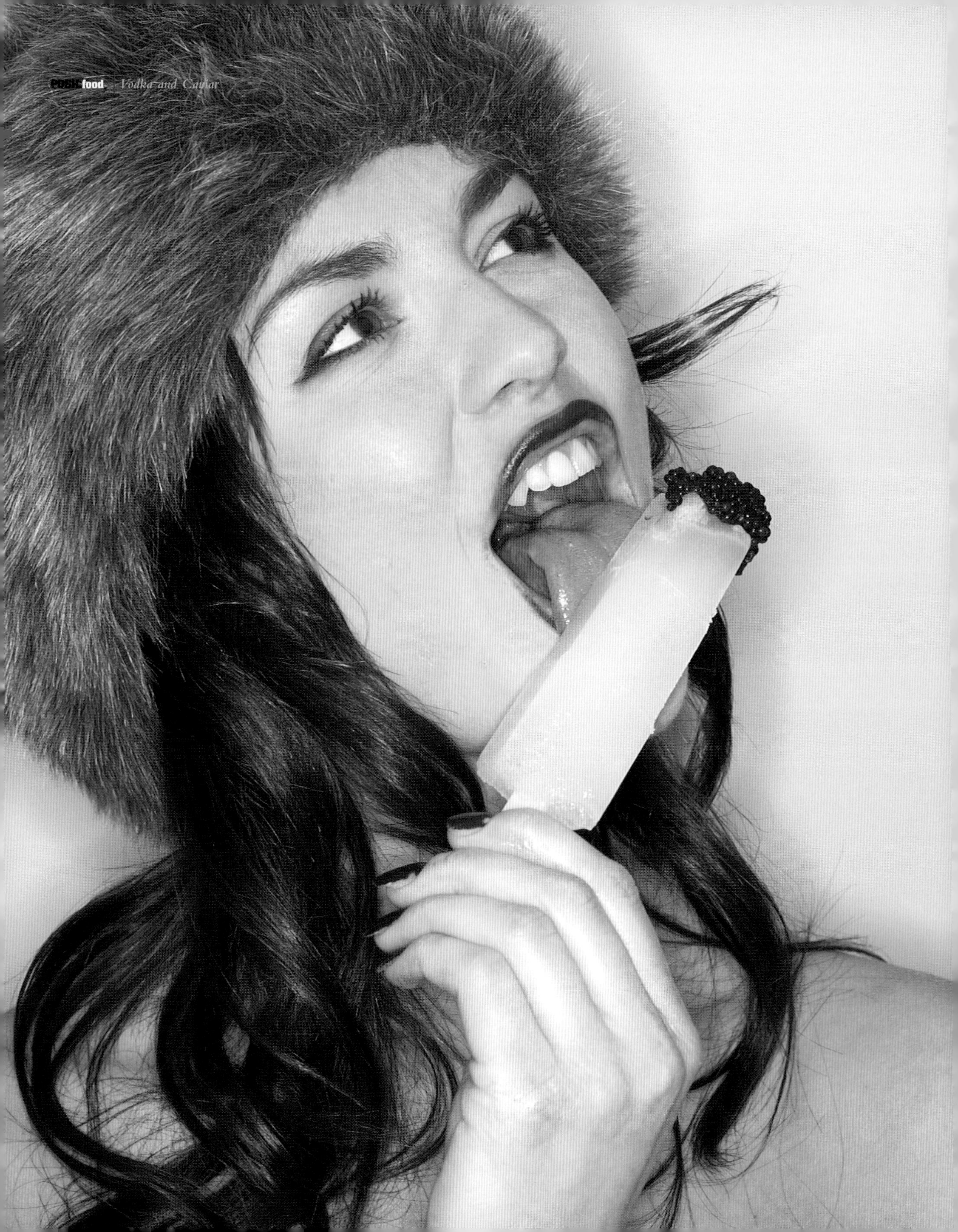

STUPID MILLIONAIRES
Vodka Ice Lollies

Serves:8

Here is what you need:

500ml   Water
300ml   Vodka
100g   Caster sugar

What you need to do to it:

1. In a pan boil the vodka, water and caster sugar.

2. Pour into lolly moulds, freeze for 24 hours.

For added stupidity, dip end of ice lolly in the best Beluga Caviar 'one' can find.

Serving suggestion see opposite.

Alternatively can be served with blinis and soured cream.

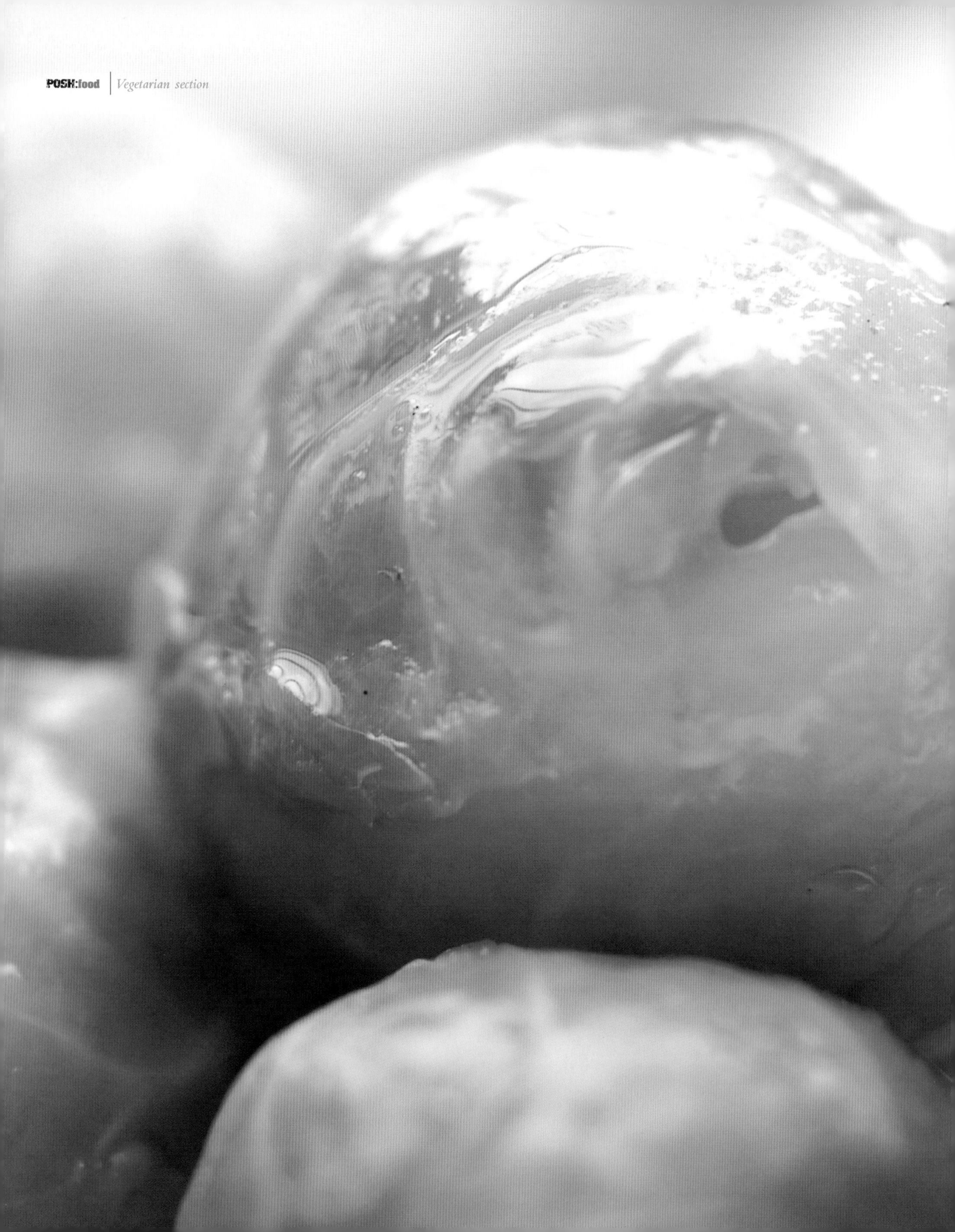

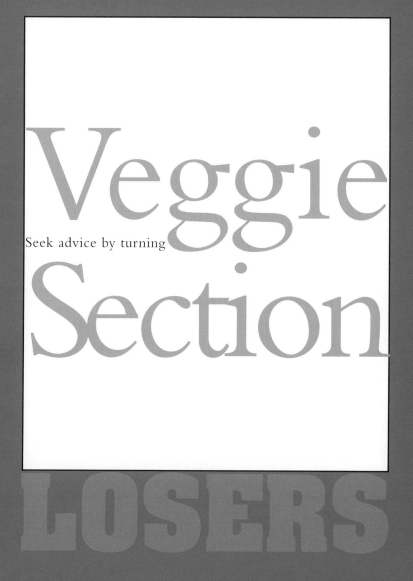

Seek advice by turning

Veggie
Section

LOSERS

Go on.
You know you want it!

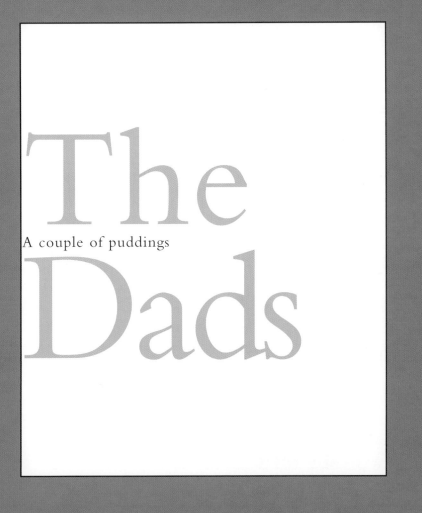

The Dads

A couple of puddings

'THE DADS'

It's January 2005. We have made it through another hectic Christmas and New Year and our contemplations turn to further merriment. The time has come to get back to Bergerac at last and to visit Monsieur Martin, the man with the truffles, and to search out his 'black gold'.

On this occasion Reevsie and I have invited our Dads to join us and to help us with our next venture. They have agreed and so with additional eagerness we continue on our gastro photo journey.

Sunday 23rd January 2005

Bergerac 'almost international' receives the four of us in the way that only Bergerac can. It's unusually cold at the moment and despite the warnings we really hadn't believed that the South West of France could actually be as bitter as this. Fiona and my Mum obviously did though, as they have packed some pretty warm gear for us – including a toasty pair of pyjamas for me, which I rarely wear at home.

Reevsie has done his own packing – Levi 501s and Fat Face jumpers – three in total – all blue and all the same (see Summer wardrobe). I don't know what Reevsie's Dad (Mike) has packed in his bag – I have only met him a few times and I don't really think I know him well enough to pry into his apparel preferences.

My Dad (John) looks snug as a bug in his suede jacket, woollen black hat, scarf and decent walking shoes.

'The Guys' as I shall now collectively refer to our Dads have gone to the baggage reclaim which only takes a couple of minutes and Chris and I are off to the de-mountable office that is the home of the rent a voiture people.

It is with some remorse that I find it necessary to convey the sad news that we have blown out our Hertz girl. Regretfully we have discovered a cheaper alternative and although Reevsie and I will miss her sweet and charming smile, we quickly get over these sombre thoughts and head towards our sparkling little red Scenic.

Our first port of call is Tony and Jane's gite again and we arrive here safely with no sign of the car shaking its ass. The short trek has been music free as the car has no cd player. No cd player means no Snow Patrol, no Haircut 100 and thankfully no bloody Nik Kershaw. Having said that even Nik is better than that groovy old Johnny Halliday who bellowed out from the second that we allowed the radio to spring into life.

The sleeping gite hasn't seen a visitor for ages but Tony leaves the heating on constantly – albeit on tick over just to keep the old place from becoming damp. Chris assures us that our home will soon become nice and warm – a welcome from the angry, snow laden skies that dawdle menacingly outside.

Wrong – the gite is still freezing, the heating is broken and even a long winded telephone conversation with Tony back home can't resolve the problem. We have now pushed every button, turned every valve and manipulated every pipe yet the hibernating monster of hidden warmth refuses to awaken.

**A funny thing just happened. I was just checking my spelling of manipulate in my dictionary when I came across the most amazing word. The word is Mangelwurzel (which is a variety of beet) I suddenly love this word and I think I want to be known as Mark Mangelwurzel. In fact if this book ever gets published I will use this as my pen name.(Prat! Ed.)*

Anyway, back to the story. We haven't planned on staying at the gite tonight so Tony suggests that we visit his neighbours (Monique and her husband) who are certain to be able to fix the problem.

Monique assures us that her husband will look into the dilemma when he returns from work.

In the meantime the four of us head down to St Alvére where we are due to meet and stay with Monsieur Martin, our truffle king.

Mike determines that this country is 'bleeding cold' and I wonder what type of work Monique's husband will be returning from. Monique is responsible for fattening the geese for the not so glorious production of foie gras.

The early evening has brought us to Truffiere de la Bergerie. A little understated sign on the outside of this rambling farm is the only hint of the treasure that is hidden somewhere in the tidy rows of planted forest behind it.

As we pull up to his charming, untidy residence Monsieur Martin moans that we are late.

Locally, Monsieur Martin is an important man. And Monsieur Martin is clearly an important man in a hurry. His face is cracked by the blistering summer heat of South Western France and the cold, bitter winter that affords him no respite. He is a dandy man with his own peculiar charm and in the corner of his mouth is a cigarette that I swear never seems to go out.

We formally introduce ourselves to him and offering us his weathered and working hand he welcomes us to his home and hurriedly gesticulates to his wife to direct us to the tiny lodge that will be our sanctuary tonight.

His wife explains that we are booked to have dinner locally and that if we don't hurry our meal will be ruined.

The lodgings are terribly rustic but adequate. As we walk across to them we are met by a noisy donkey, a whole load of well fed chickens, sheep and dogs of just about every extraction.

It's typically French – rickety old stairs that are almost impossibly steep (and that would meet no current health and safety legislation at home) lead us across a tiny landing to two bedrooms.

The bedrooms are however quite cosy as is the bathroom which is warmed by means of a fan heater, plugged in next to the shower! Amused and slightly anxious we head out for our much awaited and eagerly anticipated evening meal.

Reevsie is at the wheel and luckily Madame Martin is driving ahead of us, directing us to Sophie's home. The trek to her dwelling is alarming. Chris is panicking as we motor down the most desolate and pretty little farm tracks with the rear end of the Scenic at last shaking its ass as the tyres grapple for some kind of traction in the slippery mud.

We have decided to be proper country men and to eat in what has now become a popular form of French society – 'The Chambre d'hote', similar I suppose to our good old guest houses where local people welcome guests into their own homes. Choices are generally limited to two, – LIKE IT OR LUMP IT - and we have the feeling that we are definitely going to like it as we are cold, tired and hungry!

Sophie greets us by the door and after apologising for our tardiness we are welcomed into a sitting room with four small chairs surrounding a blistering fire. The fire is burning wood inside a metal drum with a bodged up sort of extraction unit. The almost nuclear heat has caused the drum to bubble and warp and actually glow red hot. Sophie warns us not to touch the drum and disappears into an adjoining kitchen. We rub our hands and start to melt and conclude once more that this is France after all.

Behind us is an old wooden farm table set with four places, a homely cloth and unlit candles. Everything looks perfect and these four English guys are salivating with expectation.

Sophie's home is very old and very un finished – a project we surmise that may well take many more years and lots of dinners to complete. The living room is a great confusion of old stone walls, with loads of proper wooden beams and rugs and blankets everywhere. In the corner is a sparsely yet fashionably decorated Christmas tree. This is of course the end of January after all!

As we sit thawing by the open fire the old oak door is nudged open by a handsome looking black Labrador. We are soon told that this chap is responsible for searching out the truffles buried on Sophie's land.

Behind Thor are drinks and canapés served by the two gorgeous little girls who are Sophie's daughters.

The obligatory refreshment turns out to be a huge quantity of Martinique rum to wash down the smoked salmon tasters and home made pastry cheesy straws.

I have a great love for animals, and dogs in particular and am stroking Thor, who has decided to use my lap as his pillow. Suddenly he is aggravated and turns to bite himself on the underside of his sleek body. His grunting and chewing has now resulted in a truly disgusting sight – the emergence of a horrible large, white worm, alive and boisterously trying to escape from the dog's body.

I feel completely sick and declining the cheesy straw that Mike is offering me I desperately try to persuade my fellow diners to regard the sight, so that they too would be put off any further offerings.

We all feel quite sorry for the dog, but don't deem it appropriate to embarrass Sophie as we are asked to go to the table for the upcoming feast.

Finally Chris clocks the worm and leaving him looking like he is going to heave, we take it in turns to wash our hands and make sure we make no further contact with the poor K9.

We are served with a carafe of very ordinary red wine but luckily I have a rucksack of four bottles brought all the way from home. I have adopted a policy of taking booze everywhere, as you never know when the need for a decent slurp may arise.
Sophie is only too happy for us to open our own. She enjoys a glass of Argentinean with us and discusses the merits of the local vin de table.

My Dad is a wine expert and indeed a wine buff. He seems a little happier now that the other bottles are opened. Reevsie doesn't find anything wrong with the carafe which we have now pushed firmly in front of him.

Sophie offers Reevsie another top up but he declines as he is driving this evening. Sophie begins to giggle in disbelief

"It's only a short drive" she says as she fills his glass

Again we conclude that this is France, after all.

Our hearty 'take no prisoners' dinner 'arrives. We start with a little green salad of warm duck gizzards, which, if you don't think about it too much, actually tastes quite nice. To follow, large omelettes studded with Sophie's truffles.

The black lab with the hideous creature still semi-protruding is sitting close to Chris, who in turn is desperately trying to ignore its very existence.

Desserts arrive in the form of a very good apple tart and a not so great fig tart and lucky old Thor is offered two portions of the figs which he heartily gobbles up. We have a strange premonition that the figs will in some way come back to haunt us. Reevsie is impressed by the Labrador's understanding of my French for "sit" and he has now decided to call me Barbara Woodhouse.

John and Mike are meanwhile bantering on about coinage before decimalization. Mike wants to keep the pound and English Cheeses. Chris on the other hand doesn't care.

As the conversation excitingly moves on to threepenny bits we are rescued by the presence of Sophie who now insists that French Chefs are the best in the world. She wonders if anyone would like a further slice of fig tart and happily clears the table.

Reevsie is contemplating a further photo opportunity and asks our host whether we could return tomorrow to take pictures of some truffle hunting with Thor. Sophie is happy to oblige. We thank her for her fabulous hospitality and on leaving I insist that Chris should stroke the dog, explaining to Sophie his great love of all animals.

We have accorded Chris the smallest bed, as he is the smallest bloke. Mike has the privilege of his own room as we are informed that he can snore for England. Dad and I just crash out in the other two beds in a happy and tipsy disposition.

The rumour is true. That bloke can snore for England, France, in fact Europe and possibly the world. Between him, the bloody donkey and all sorts of other farmyard noises, our 7am alarm took no time to come around.

Poor old Chris is complaining that his body hurts as his bed was so small he couldn't move all night, Mike is happy and rested, John is on top form and I'm somewhere in the middle.

There is a certain camaraderie building up between four blokes, as we take it in turns to take a sort of shower, being careful not to drip on the exposed fan heater.

The morning is frosty and crisp. The sky looks snowy and the chickens are hungry. The donkey bids us bonjour with an eeaaaw and not for the first time we ingest the true beauty of this rustic, homely land. It's just so quiet and the air that hits the back of your throat is so clear of pollution that you can taste sweetness.

We have agreed to meet Monsieur Martin at the truffle market, a few kilometres from here in St Alvére. We are gagging for coffee, as regretfully there is no facility for us visitors to make it at the dwelling during this quieter time of the year.

Dad John is a little upset that there is no confiture to accompany our warm croissants, while I find this an odd but charming trait of our French cousins.

It's equally strange that French markets offer an unparalleled choice of fantastic vegetables for sale – yet they so rarely actually appear as an accompaniment to a main course. I suppose that vegetables are more akin to peasant food which–yes - makes all of us English Peasants!

Never mind, we are once more warm and cosy. We notice that this café also has a fully decorated Christmas tree in the corner of the room. We really should ask why they are still celebrating the festive season at this time of the year, and pledge to pose the question.

Next to the artificial Christmas fir is a shelf full of magazines for sale. This café obviously plays host to International Travellers as above the rack there is a sign saying in English "Please don't read the newspapers." W.H Smith – please take note.

Reevsie's shooting hand seems to have thawed out and he's snapping away in earnest; here, there and everywhere. Often you forget he's taking photos. He vanishes and the next thing you know he has taken a great picture of you picking your nose (or worse).

St Alvére is another of those sleepy little French hamlets. It's snowing, the Christmas lights and decorations are still up and there is a real air of excitement as we spot the covered truffle market where already a generous handful of locals is gathering outside.

We have found a warm and well used café, starting to fill with all types of characters. There are farmers in dirty wellies with filthy hands mixing happily with Parisian city slickers – they must be buyers or brokers - and in the corner a gaggle of Englishmen earnestly supping mugs full of luscious, body kicking, tar–like coffee.

The queue of locals outside the truffle market has now expanded. A glance through the windows exposes an interior with a dozen or so traders standing erectly behind their trestle tables. Upon theses tables are proudly positioned truffles of a million different sizes, hues and shapes – all waiting for buyers, traders or restaurateurs to make their bids.

It seems that the inside of the market is occupied by the important people, all keeping nice and warm. On the outside are us lesser mortals, due to be granted entry into this magical Kingdom from 10am when it is open to the public, who shall be allowed to purchase the remnants or the crumbs left by the influential and prominent purchasers. Until then you may look and wish.

Today though WE ARE IMPORTANT because we know Monsieur Martin. Armed with this priceless connection we brush past the locals full of apologies, and are immediately confronted by a gentleman of the French truffle police clearly placed 'on the door' to banish any premature or forbidden entry.

We let the sentry know that we are particularly good friends of his master and cautiously he allows us to pass.

Once inside we are almost greeted by the God of truffles. The cigarette hanging from the side of his mouth seems to have actually extinguished as he cracks open a slight smile. He allows us to oscillate amongst his people and to learn about his precious fungus.

It's all a bit embarrassing really. These local people know so much about their produce; they describe to us the differences in smell, taste and texture. I wonder how many people living near me would be so knowledgeable about asparagus, for example, which grows in the fields around my village, and I become aware that I know nothing about truffles at all.

Suddenly there is a slap of hands and a hush as Monsieur Martin stands up to make a speech. The whole indoor market is enveloped in silence as this clever man sets the price of the truffles based on current global trends. The market traders urgently set about penning prices on bits of paper and the deal is done.

There is a slight interruption as one of the lessers tries to break through the ranks and enter the building. He is quickly ejected.

We are learning loads and it seems that despite a rather average season the price has been set at around 700 to 800 euros per kilo. No wonder the traders are smiling.

Monsieur Martin is now sending round a perfectly formed white truffle from Italy. We are told to look at it in its box, to smell it but not to touch. The price of this little lump of fungus has been set to a monstrous 4000 euros per kilo. The French are experiencing near orgasmic palpitations as they sniff the aroma of the truffle. Reevsie turns his nose up, I'm not impressed and as for the guys, well they're talking golf!

Chris is taking more photos. Truffles and money are changing hands all around us and we suddenly have a great idea about doing a book in Italy (while looking for truffles of course).

But first things first, I am going to make a pizza. This pizza will be really special. It will be spilling with truffles and foie gras and of course this one will be designed for our Stupid Millionaires range!

I negotiate a very poor deal with one of the vendors and choose three of the black things for the pizza. We shall need to get some tomatoes, cheese, flour and foie gras.

It must be 10am as the doors of the market have sprung open and the room is mobbed by urgent locals desperate to clean up with the remaining offerings.

We buy some vegetables and a few other bits and notice a nice restaurant open for luncheon. A hearty bowl of Paysanne soup (that's where the vegetables go then) and a hunk of decent bread help to quench our continental hunger. It is here that we decide the making of the pizza and John and Mike conclude that 11am is certainly not too early for a glass of wine. Reevsie and I concur and begin to understand the drinking habits of our dads!

We're back with Monsieur Martin for a tour of his woodland. He really is massively knowledgeable about his art – and he's still in a hurry.

There is a so much to learn about truffles and so much conspiracy with nature is necessary for these rarities to grow.

Monsieur Martin's truffles are sort of harvested in particular woods which are planted out with beech and oak trees. The roots of these trees, the spores, the leaves, the season, the warmth, the rain, the heat and the cold must all come together at the right time to yield one decent little truffle. Then it has to grow to the correct size before it rots and all that's got to be done before you send your dog out to try and find it!

Monsieur Martin waxes lyrical about his life with real passion then complains that he is financially poor.

We wonder how this is possible when he has set a selling price for his truffles at almost 800 euros a kilo.

Father John is chatting to a man who seems to have infiltrated our little group. It transpires that he is a German journalist writing for a glossy magazine. He is also here to gain information about the black gold and Dad seems to have successfully brokered a deal for Reevsie to sell him some of his photos!

The German must have a great memory as I can't spot a note book and with no camera of his own, I wonder what calibre of glossy magazine he actually contributes to!

Monsieur Martin finishes his tour with one of his scruffy little dogs successfully finding some undersized truffles.

We thank him and pay him for our accommodation. Monsieur Martin is still in a hurry, but not that much of a hurry. Before bidding us farewell he counts the money twice.

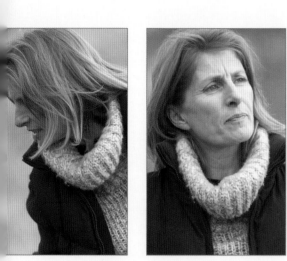

This pattern is repeated many times and poor old Sophie can't understand why her dog is so full of beans and so disobedient today. She tells us that Thor never behaves so badly and wonders if it something he has eaten!

Again he runs off in the direction of the truffle scent. This time he begins to forage in an area with definite expectancy. Chris and I run behind him and Sophie bends down to see what he has discovered. Then it happens. Chris and I are subjected to the most enormous, canine fart that we have ever heard, followed by the entire fig tart being ejected from the poor chap's bottom.

It absolutely stinks and Reevsie and I are standing down wind of the foul stench. I had a feeling that tart would come back to haunt us. And now we know why the poor dog was misbehaving.

We climb yet more hills and cross more cornfields and eventually find success. Thor begins to scratch an area on the ground and lo and behold he discovers one truffle, then another, then another.

Sophie has got her truffles, Chris has got his pictures and Thor has got the shits.

Returning back to the car Chris and I walk upwind of the stinking hound. We have had a great day and we are laughing like school kids!

Laughing is such great therapy and we both comment that we haven't had this much fun for years.

We've been a bit longer than the promised half an hour and the dads seem just a little peeved with us. But we rejoice on hearing the news that Monique has called and the heating at the gite is mended. What a great day!

Back up the road we arrive once again at Sophie's. Luckily she has remembered we are coming and she greets us like long lost friends.

A blizzard is approaching and the Dads have decided to remain within the comfort confines of the little Scenic while Reevsie and I follow Sophie and Thor through one cornfield into the next. The Dads are bound to be having a meaningful conversation and in any case we should only be about half an hour.

Sophie orders the black lab (now free from worms) to "serche les truffes" and wagging his tail he runs off deliberately in the direction of the hidden treasure. He finds a spot by a mature oak tree where he barks, digs manically with his front paws and discovers …. a stone!

Thor is ordered to continue his search.

LOVELY, ISN'T IT?

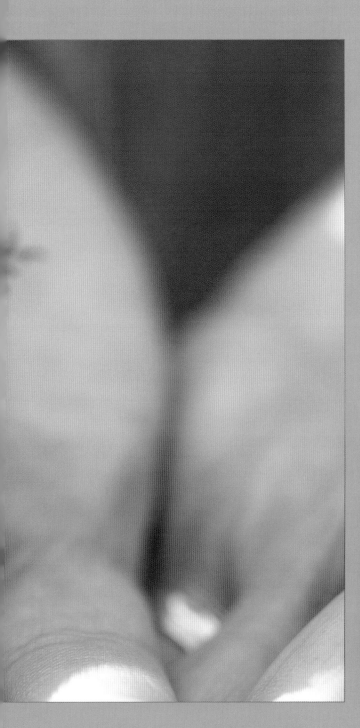

We have actually been so long that Father John is busting for a wee. He can however wait, as the journey to the gite should only take 20 minutes. Let's face it, it's 'bleeding cold' out there.

On arrival at the gite, it turns out that Father John can't wait after all. Reevsie is taking an age to open the damp front door and Dad runs into the hedge to relieve himself. This is France, after all.

Eventually we enter the gite and are heartily dismayed to discover that the heating is only just tepid. In fact our little farmhouse is still positively brass monkeys.

Never mind, it should soon warm up. After downloading a quantity of photos and drinking a decent glass of local wine, we decide to head down to Cadouin to visit our old friend's delightful pizza place.

The short journey has been made more exciting this evening - and more dangerous by the astounding sight of four large deer standing boldly in the middle of the road.

As I am the wheel man tonight I make a mental note that there are sheer drops on both sides of this windy road and no fences to prevent an ass shaking Scenic from crashing down the steep hills.

The strangely serene and handsome creatures trot off, and we are left wondering why they choose to congregate on this particular road when there are millions of acres of open space to play on.

The pizza place is closed and typically at dinner time, here in off-season France, so is every other eating house.

A decision is reached to visit a super bistro in Tremolat, a fair distance up the road. As it turns out, a super bistro with a not so super restaurant manager. Its 6.30pm when we arrive, and it's already freezing outside as we enter this welcoming abode. The manager unhappily slouches towards us and nonchalantly asks us what we want

"Un table á quatre, sil vous plait" we reply.

Unimpressed with our French, Monsieur le Toss, responds that the Bistro is not open until 7pm, and that we shall have to come back later. Now as I said, it's freezing outside and with nowhere else to go (except for the little car) we ask if we may take a seat here in the warmth – until the desired time.

Le Toss shrugs his shoulders and meanders of to a well laid table or two where he is joined by His Royal Highness the Chef de Bistro.

The two staff begin their meal with a tasty looking entrée which is followed by what looks to be a particularly nice looking main course. Sadly we are offered no pre-dinner drinks or canapés while we are waiting. In truth we are made to feel pretty unwelcome.

Please don't get me wrong. I, more than most people, understand Restaurants and the attitude of Restaurant staff. Of course it is important for the staff to sit down and enjoy their food, but this bloke is really taking the piss.

I tell the guys who work with me always remember to the importance of our guests. We invariably try to present a 'human face' and display understanding when dealing with our guests.

In my Restaurant, if clients happen to arrive before we are open, we would explain that they have caught us on the hop. We would offer them a drink and a little appetizer and we would keep them warm! We would then let the client know that we are just eating our dinner and that we will be happy to look after them as soon as we're back on duty. There you have it, everyone happy!

Monsieur le Toss has no such consideration, no manners. It's now ten past seven and as he lights his second fag I have a great desire to thump him! However one should never advocate violence and, besides, the food here looks good.

At last we are seated and now the Manager seems a little happier (you see the way to a man's heart). In fact, the supercilious little prat is trying to have a conversation with us in his almost perfect English.

Reevsie and I wait for him to explain certain dishes and then look at each other perplexedly - playing the game that we haven't understood what he was saying as his English was not really up to scratch - and with more than a little air of embarrassment our Manager serves us with a rather decent meal.

As it happens we are one of only two tables of customers this evening. The other is occupied by two wealthy looking women speaking a language that is difficult to place. We munch through egg mayonnaise, Cod boulangere, a decent duck confit and delicious cheeses. The conversation between the guys has now turned to Masonic lodges and the War years.

I glance over at Chris who has by now had a glass of red too many. His complexion is ruddy (like his hair) and his eyes are starting to close. The conversation has caused the poor lad to lose his will to live.

It's getting late, the other table of two has long gone, and Monsieur le Toss is hovering around our table, gently persuading us that it is now time for us to depart. Clearly this man is suddenly in a hurry to get home. Ordering more coffee, we wonder if we could have just a little more cheese?

Each time we look across we can see that he is fed up and waiting for us to request the bill but we remember what it's like being made to wait and determine that revenge really is a dessert best served cold.

Eventually we bid farewell to Monsieur le Toss who in turn had bade farewell to a tip and we quickly try to warm ourselves in the snug cabin of our little Scenic. Truthfully though the food had been great and we were later to find out that this front of house chap was due to leave the Bistro and had therefore clearly lost all interest in being there.

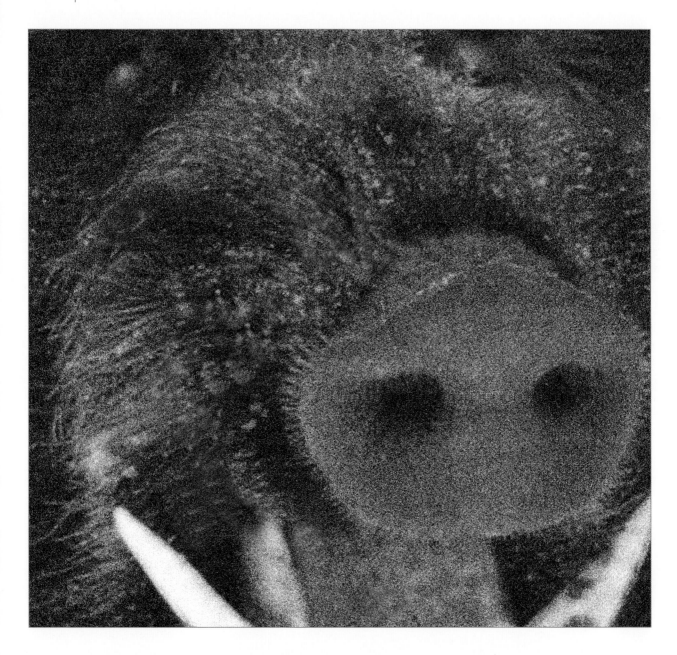

The temperature outside is -4 degrees, but the interior is warming rapidly thanks to the efficient heating system of this little red voiture. It is true that French cars are built more for comfort than looks.

The little car skids and with the sound of four seat belts urgently locking into place, slides to a rude stop. The language in the car is interesting as we have just encountered a near death experience courtesy of the biggest, dirtiest great wild boar we have ever had the misfortune to witness in our lives.

The mammoth beast ran from one side of the road to the other. The headlights obviously startled him and we missed him by inches.

A second or so earlier would have seen us wearing the prehistoric pig, the car would certainly have been totalled and there is every chance you would not be reading this now. (For which you might be profoundly grateful.)

At home we live in the country. It's not unusual to see wild creatures running about at night. But the sight of this menacing looking porker full of neck and muscle, with great tusks and little eyes staring menacingly at us, is one of the most frightening things I have encountered on a road anywhere in the world!

Thanking God, I nervously engage first gear and we slowly continue our drive home. The conversation in the back has reverted to golf.

Reevsie has pulled out the Dictaphone we are using as a diary and he is muttering something about a "FUCKING MONSTER". This time I don't think he is talking about his mother in law.

Monique has failed in her mission. The gite is still cold. The radiators are at best only tepid almost like they need bleeding. But in truth they don't as there is still something fundamentally amiss with the central heating system.

Bed seems to be the most sensible option. A great camaraderie between the four of us now exists and on retiring the chat has turned to quotes from Scott of the Antarctic "I'm going to bed Reevsie, I may be some time"

I don't wear pyjamas in bed. I'm a boxer short and T shirt type of guy – but thank God Fiona has packed me some thermal ones on this freezing night.

Dad has nestled himself up and is trying to keep himself warm as best as possible in his sleeping bag which is covered with blankets and even his coat. When he talks to me I can see his breath, yet he is in excellent spirits and I am enjoying some proper quality time with him. Chris and Mike have bedded down in the other bedroom which seems to be a little warmer as they have a bigger radiator, although to be fair it's hardly knocking out nuclear heat (and Mike does snore a bit too).

I undress as quickly as possible and dig into my bag to grab the jim jams Fiona has packed for me. I pull them on and suddenly realise something awful. They're not mine, they are Fiona's.

They are two foot short and very tight but they do give me quite a lunch box and I conceive that I actually quite like wearing them! Anyway, there's no way I'm taking them off as I need every bit of heat and - apart from my jeans - I have nothing else to wear.

Just then there's a knock at the door and before I can utter the words "just a minute", Reevsie has walked in and found me - yep, you've guessed - it in my wife's bed wear. He had thoughtfully brought us a little fan heater and is now laughing so loudly, that he has woken my Dad up.

Together they look at me and no amount of excuses will vindicate me of this ghastly crime. I text Fiona with the funny news that she has inadvertently got me into some trouble and even my wife doesn't text back!

They say you end up like your parents. That's fine in many way's but bloody hell, I hope I don't end up snoring as loud as my dad, at his age or any. I think the wife might agree with me on that.

The first night we banished him to the spare room and still heard him, tonight he's in with me. I have a hood over my head, a thick four seasons sleeping bag and a hat with furry ears on and I can still hear the sound of thunder from the bed next to me.

It must be five in the morning and the house is just becoming warm with a very small 'w'. My breath is still visible. I really need sleep, I can't hear any noise in the adjoining room. Mark must have smothered his father already? Probably with his wife's pyjamas!

I awake realising that I must have finally slept. There's a lot of sun coming through the window, I scrabble to take a look, Fantastic – it's a glorious and sunny morning, great photography weather. Even better Dad has stopped snoring, Oh no, maybe I spoke too soon! The 7am from Bergerac has just left the station.

I make my way to the kitchen to make the tea, Mark's already there, we both look shattered. Both Dads on the other hand, look well rested and jovial, I wonder why!

I'm going to do some photos outside while the others attempt a shower with freezing cold water, I decline for as much as its sunny outside its still only above freezing and I don't want to freeze my head while taking pictures. Meanwhile Mark's going to prepare the pizza bases before we head off for breakfast.

It only takes Fifteen minutes and Mr Baumann junior joins me in the cold with a look of resignation, on his face "your idea" I get in quickly. "No your idea." comes the reply. "shut up and look chef like while I take you photo." I was getting some shots of the gite with a pile of wood in the foreground, I stick Mark up against the honey coloured walls rather like a firing squad and tell him to smile, something he switches on easily enough, being a veteran of numerous magazine and newspaper articles, I've noticed they seem to be more genuine when he's doing the book. We can't stay out here all day. We have food to cook, photos to take, fathers to keep out of mischief. The roles have definitely been reversed.

We decide to give the Dads a job. John writes the recipe as Mark dictates and my Dad becomes kitchen assistant. As he stirs, pours and fetches, I just take photos as usual!

The dough is left in a bowl on the radiator and we go off to Beaumont for strong coffee and freshly baked croissants. The cold hits me as soon as we go back outside but the beautiful, sunny day makes up for any discomfort from the biting chill.

Our usual café is open and we hurry inside and order "Quatre grands café au laits from madame." Mark then remembered we have to buy croissants from the bakers and disappears off to get our breakfast. I can't imagine you being able to bring food into a café in England but it's a refreshing change. I think it's the first time I've felt warm since we've been in France.

On Mark's return we tuck into the coffee and pastries until work (if you can call it that) rears its head and off we go shopping for supplies. Foie gras from the butcher's wife and coffee and milk for the old boys.

The morning is a whirlwind of stirring, blanching, rolling and explaining to both Dads that it doesn't matter that we don't have a rolling pin – an empty bottle will do. There are, I surmise, enough to go round!

We get the Dads to make their own pizzas, then one for the photo. This way it gets everyone occupied while I prepare my brick wall as a backdrop. I find it very useful to get both Dads to hold mirrors and reflect sunlight onto my subject. This is usually a job for Mark but revelling in his new found freedom he's pretending to be Cartier Bresson with my Leica!

Time is moving fast and after cleaning the gite we pack up for what is, in my opinion, the main event. Le Vieux Logis.

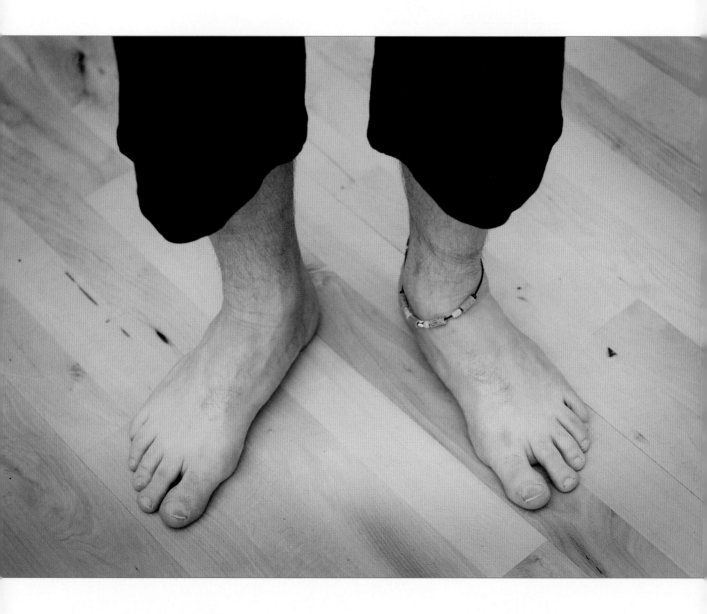

Estelle meets us always looking happy at reception. Surely it can't be because we're here?

She takes us through to see Vincent in the kitchen. Mark and him embrace and theatrically talk French like old pals. It's usually at this point I just drift away rather than grin like an idiot not understanding a word, something my wife will understand as I have done this with her family for a number of years (grin like an idiot that is).

Luckily for me (the lazy foreigner) Vincent has learnt a bit of English and as we talk about the truffle market he proudly shows us a basket, or perhaps, bucket would be more apt, of truffles.

"Five kilos in total." he proclaims,
"Nice" we say in unison,
like it's some girl's arse.

"We bought two."
"Two kilos ?" comes the reply.
"No, two!" He laughs and tells us of his ideas for our dinner. I get the impression that when one Master Chef cooks for another it becomes a special event. Fireworks happen in the kitchen. The fallout for me and the Dads is we are in for a real treat.

"Just out of interest what did you use your truffles for?"
"Oh, we made a pizza." we reply.

We leave the kitchen full of hysterical Frenchman who are now on the floor, Mark and I decide we're just too cutting edge!

Just then we meet Freddie. The owner has requested our presence. Bugger, we've been rumbled. All four of us are taken back to reception where upon our arrival, a very distinguished, older gentleman appears. He seems genuinely pleased to see us and obviously commands respect from his staff. I should mention that before we came out Mark and I sent Freddie a couple of framed photos of the hotel. The owner Monsieur Giraudel clasps my hands, happy as Larry, and talks enthusiastically in French. Freddie translates what he can but Monsieur isn't stopping for catch up. He compares the photos to a Rembrandt and starts talking about parts of a woman's body! I turn to Mark and ask "What bloody photos did you post, because I don't think they were mine!"

To cut a long story short, he's pleased with what we are doing and everybody's smiling at me, which I find very disconcerting. My Dad's beaming as only dads can and Mark's laughing, enjoying, watching me go red and mouthing the words "Golden Balls" This changes throughout the evening and evolves into Ginger Bollocks after several bottles of wine and a calvados.

Dad retires to our room and I take a quick photo of Vincent and truffles with Mark, before retiring for a snooze before dinner. So do Mark and John but reading Mark's notes it says something entirely different! I quote "The Reevsies retire to their room for a rest. While the Baumanns go for a run and do press ups before dinner!" Clearly the Baumanns have decided to make this a work of fiction!!

There are many pleasures in life, but few are as good as the anticipation of a good meal surrounded by good friends.

We sit in front of a large, roaring fire, in a snug part of the dining room. John is a formidable wine expert so he chooses our entertainment. We partake of the local Bergerac wine. The first of many appears and we all agree it's going to be a good night.

Our waiter is called Yves. He turns out to be impeccable – a knowledgeable waiter and an Arsenal fan. "Ahh, the French national team." we sigh. Still, he doesn't believe Mark when he recounts his giant boar story. He obviously thinks it's British Mickey taking!

Menus arrive, but we are told Vincent would like to surprise us with a special Truffle menu. How can we refuse? The first of NINE COURSES duly arrives.

Words cannot express how good the meal is. I think I even took photos before each course (sorry I can't help it, even Mark started to do it!) Highlights have to be: apple and celery soup with grilled scallop, mango ravioli and pork stuffed with truffles. All of them were superb. Our taste buds are in overload. Yves, now a mind reader brings Mark and I two beers while the Dads start another bottle of vin rouge.

A round of coffees and chocolates and we retire to the lounge complete with fire, to relive the experience.

Vincent visits us before he leaves and talks of taking a trip to England. He is duly invited to the Brasserie in Coggeshall and to an Arsenal match – if we can get tickets?

It's now midnight and both Dads head up to their rooms happy, if a little the worse for wear!

Mark and I talk over the last few days discussing how good it's been: the truffle market, making our Dads eat Stupid Millionaires' pizza outside in the middle of January, hunting for truffles with Sophie and best of all the meal at The Shed. All this and the obligatory conversations about putting the world to rights.

Tomorrow morning we head back to Blighty and back to work. Our book may appear to finish here but the journey continues. More photography, testing recipes to destruction, talking with agents, publishers and overloading Neil our designer with more information than he ever wanted in his life. This in fact has been the easy bit, the rest, well that's another book !

Our quest though has been fulfilled and it ends as we hoped, Mark Baumann Chef and Chris Reeve photographer, content with their work, life, lot, even if it is for just one day.

Until the next stupid idea !

STACK
A BOX

HOMEBASE

DURABLE, STACK OR NEST STORAGE BOX
CO-ORDINATING LIDS AVAILABLE

MOPPING UP
THE DIRTY JOB OF DESIGNING THE BOOK!

A WORD FROM OUR SPONSOR:

Neil Hatton: Designer of book and basic bullshit filter.

The Third leg.

If my memory is correct I was introduced into this little project as three frustrated 'creatives', top of our profession with only our super stardom and its high earnings avoiding us. A tripod of authority. A chef, a photographer and me, the designer, creating a no-punches cook book, answerable to no man not in our triangle of power!

A project to buck the trend by not following it, creating a cook book for us.

Three fellas giving their best to beat 'the man' and produce a book which would gain respect without selling out (rather than pass its sell-by-date!). No ordinary cook book; a book for men, real men who sweat, swear and occasionally disobey their partners !

Who were we kidding? You know by now, you've read this far, right? Your impressions so far are of a frustrated chef and ginger photographer having a couple of jollies around France (really roughing it, not!) and in between the saucy Hertz car hire lady and the rancid dog tales you are offered fine cuisine, presented beautifully in colour and instruction.

Occasionally forgetting the mission statement of our 'real men' status, quickly slipping in images of scantly clad women because that's what you want (or is that what we wanted you to want?) to re-assure our directive.

Weeks of photography, a month in France, two months of discussion and two years of designing, we have the book at a near completed state.

I remind myself of the tripod analogy, not too sure how it all worked out. You're holding a book of about 224 pages and this is the first you have heard from me. Page 220, the third leg, never leaving the country, indeed rarely leaving this bloody laptop to design and redesign this testament from the heavens of the oven. Just my luck to come into the project after all the fun has been had. It's rather like having the winning lottery numbers minus the ticket!

My intention from the very start was to take a back seat in the forefront of what really is the Mark and Reevsie show, made pretty by me! My only rule that I take no orders from anyone in regards to the layout or its design, but will two columns be OK due to the readability of 10pt Bembo on 14pt leading?

But I think this much absence is hard to justify in a book I now call my own.

The plan for my content was potentially to give a third party account of the other two. To give what you have read and digested more realism, a level account of the real chef and his photographer. Strangely the story so far is pretty accurate in its illustration of how they both think and function.

Perhaps a little inside information on my first (and potentially last) impressions of them might just strengthen the cause.

I have known Reevsie the longer. In a nutshell the complete ying to my yang (note no homosexual gags needed here!). The half empty to my half full. Reevsie is only happy when he is sad; no complexity to him, just straight 'A' miserable sod. Once referred to by me as a mood vacuum, but let me quickly add that I have never met someone who can make anyone feel as relaxed, welcome and smile like Reevsie. He manages to put people at ease, possibly by making them aware 'whatever their problems are they can't be as bad his' tactics which always win them over. Always offering to lend a hand (when it's not connected to his true love, the camera).

It's at this point that I should say that I love, nay adore, his photos. He can make a blessed bathroom tap look like an arm of God. He may see life as doom and gloom (and that's just his wardrobe) but through the viewfinder he makes you realise what amazing beauty there is right in front of you (if only we had a lens filter to see it). A true artist, although he won't admit it (that would be too gay)! Rarely touching up his images on his trusty computer, he relies on natural skill (as well as colour temperature and the physics of light, or so he tells me!).

I can honestly say that no picture in this book has been touched up (except for the models, but they had it coming) which is a testament to his skill. Hopefully this book will wake people up to his talent (and perhaps a few book deals!).

His attempt at being a geezer; a real, blokey, bloke, bloke will sadly never happen. I'm as close as he's going to get to working class (hence my 'common friend' tag). But you can't knock his desire to legitimately take photos of prime totty by calling it a cook book for blokes. There is method to his madness.

Which nicely leads me to Mark, who actually looks mad. His hair has a mind of its own but always looks slightly confused, like a startled sheep. Needless to say he always looks 'trendy'. He stands over you like an undersized giant, not tall enough to own his own beanstalk, but who has slayed the golden egg laying goose because it looked tasty.

A no-nonsense chef who could squeeze the air out of a fly's lung and serve it as an award winning meal, even with his bear like paws. Delicate in his hearing yet loud in thought. His lust for art and culture is apparent in the surroundings of his restaurant and wardrobe. The walls covered with an eclectic collection of paintings and sketches and his back covered with scary shirts and dodgy ankle bracelets (very suspect). He towers over the preparation table like a cat waiting to pounce on a unsuspecting bird, bashing and mashing food and presenting it like a piece of delicate art. A desire burns deep within Mark which is infectious, I think it's just a matter of time before he is discovered and stretched over our flat TV screens like a Channel 4 wet dream. Challenging and conflicting but always seeming to have a voice of reason. I was introduced to his food first, then the man, visiting his restaurant when luck fell my way. I'm a simple man who doesn't like hoity toity people and their hoity toity food (much to Reevisie's disgust and enjoyment), so going to fancy restaurants always left a bad taste in my mouth.

Baumanns however is where top class food and top class atmosphere don't mean you have to be intimidated by the maitre d' (indeed Greg is a very nice man - potentially homosexual)), let alone the menu. The food served is always top notch and the imaginary stories told off the walls are always a source of conversation. So when being asked by Reevsie whether I would be interested in making a cookbook with Mark I jumped at the chance, if only to meet him.

Surprisingly for someone so talented, he rarely talks of his gift, always finding what you do more interesting. This is very unusual, most people can't wait to tell you how talented and successful they are.

Always pleased to see you and deliberate in his farewells, his mad look disappears into even more of a BFG (not to be confused with his mean BLT!).

The common thread between the two rascals is they are indeed incredibly talented people with only the woes of life that get them down. Basically 'Every other bugger out there who is half as talented is living the dream. Why aren't we?' Hence the Posh food cook book was born.

Now I'm not totally sure where I fit into all of this. One would like to think that they asked me because I stand for the core values I have just spoken about in my own life. A desire to create thought provoking design that inspires people and possibly gain a nod of excellence for all my hard efforts and constant push to better myself, I think the chances are they didn't know any other bugger who would give up two years of design and artwork for free!

Needless to say my constant ideas and suggestions have been listened to, laughed at and then put into action, so maybe we all do have something in common. Get this bloody book finished and printed so we can get on with our lives (until the next project!).

On with the show!!!

With thanks to:

The 'Information Architect' - Neil Hatton. Third leg of the tripod and partner in our little excursion. The guy who has had all the shit without the fun! Rarely photographed outside his cage, as rare a designer as the proverbial hen's teeth!

The Editor - Richard Evers. For agreeing to edit and knock about something that would frighten mere mortals and for being so polite over Mark's spelling and Chris's grammar. and Neil's ability to write pure gold. *(Ed: that should be total bollocks).*

The Wives - for letting us off the hook.
Adéle (Neil's fiancée) for letting him work on the book.
The Dads - for always being right!
The Mums - for letting them off the hook.
Michele (the mother-in-law) – for letting us steal her posh plates and cutlery.
Tony (father-in-law) & Jane –for letting us squat in the gite.

The Stupid Millionaires - for being really stupid millionaires.
The French for being French and making the English feel superior.
Fredric "Freddie"- the perfect host.
Vincent 'Vinnie' for suffering two Englishmen in his kitchen.
Estelle for speaking perfect English.
Sofia and daughters for helping find truffles.
Andrew 'Golden Boy' Reeves.
Monsieur Giraudel - Perfect gentlemen and owner of the Shed.

Mr Martin for letting us into the dark and dangerous world of 'Le Truffle'.
Luigi & Lilly and all the other agents for the honest advice!
Rachel for licking the plate so enthusiastically.
Moonie for being a game girl.
Rosie for looking glamorous at such short notice.
Jade for being a sumptuous French tart.
Hannah for making the girls look glam.
CJ, Greg and the rest of the boys and girls in the restaurant for indulging us over the last two years.
Clare for putting up with Mark and me mucking up the studio and spending far too much time and money.
Sue and Sharon for all the donkey work that I'm too stupid to do.
BarberJackson.com for allowing their 'player' to play without pay for someone else.
Lee Crisis - for *that* touch-up.
Paolo di Bacardi - for helping us search for the Holy Grail.
Jenny at effective PR for doing what PR people do.
PrintWright of Ipswich for printing this book so beautifully.

*and finally....*Helvetica!

BAUMANNHATTONREEVE

In no particular order!

Photo by Clara Barberini. Styled by Paolo di Baiardi.

www.baumannsbrasserie.com

www.reevebanks.co.uk

www.barberjackson.com

Please note that this entire book, including travel, photography, design, printing, indeed everything has been self-funded with no financial help (or belief) from any book publishers. Let's hope they are wrong and our pocket money wasn't wasted!

Any mistakes you may find in this book are entirely accidental (we only checked it 1'000 times!). We never claimed to be Shakespeare.

Obviously, we hope you have enjoyed our first adventure into the cook book world. It's success or otherwise will determine whether we can do another (that and our partners not leaving us). There are certainly a few more ideas knocking around, but I guess you'll have the final say!

We sincerely thank you all.

Disclaimer:
No animal was hurt in the production of this book, except those that were killed, cooked and eaten.

Good Food
Bad Intentions